New South Wales Mathematics Syllabus

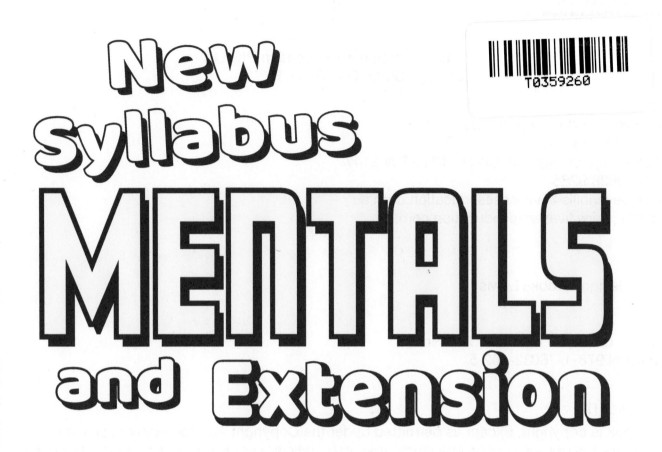

New Syllabus MENTALS and Extension

Paul Nightingale

STAGE ONE
BOOK 1

A
FIVE SENSES
PUBLICATION

———— A ————
FIVE SENSES
PUBLICATION

Copyright © 2022 Paul Nightingale - Five Senses Education Pty. Ltd.
New Syllabus Mentals and Extension - Stage One Book 1

Published by:
Five Senses Education Pty Ltd.
ABN: 16 001 414 437
2/195 Prospect Highway Seven Hills NSW 2147
Ph: 02 9838 9265
email: sevenhills@fivesenseseducation.com.au
website: www.fivesenseseducation.com.au

Cover Design: Brooke Lewis

National Library of Australia Card No.
and ISBN 978-1-76032-402-5

New Syllabus Mentals and Extension – STAGE ONE BOOK 1

About this Book for the Teacher

New South Wales Mathematics K-2 Syllabus has been developed to help raise the standard of mathematics in the first three years of formal schooling. This book, *New Syllabus Mentals and Extension Book 1* reinforces and extends the activities introduced in *New Syllabus Maths, Stage One Book 1*. Work in this book can also be used for homework but its main focus is on extension of the foundation introduced in the new syllabus.

Content and suggested activities are an extension of the syllabus guidelines and topics introduced and addressed in *New Syllabus Maths, Stage One Book 1*. Topic headings treat and develop content under these guidelines which include Number and Algebra, Measurement and Space as well as Statistics and Data.

Some additional topics have been added as Optional Extension to the Syllabus. These include Money, Angles, Lines, Open Shapes and The Metre.

While the teacher can select topics and content from any page in this book, it is suggested mental and extension activity topics follow on from topic content addressed in *New Syllabus Maths, Stage One Book 1*.

New Syllabus and Extension, Stage One Book 1 supports *New Syllabus Maths, Stage One* books with additional activities, a variety of extensions and further exposure to concepts and knowledge needed to be successful in Maths.

A full set of answers is provided at the back of the book to assist students, teachers and parents.

Message to Parents

School introduces the child to knowledge, skills and learning experiences needed to be successful in the classroom and at school. However, it is the parents who nurture a child from birth establishing values, attitudes and encouragement for the child to be a good family member and a good citizen.

It is when the teacher and parent work together to reinforce the proficiencies, experience and knowledge learned at school, with the attitudes and values of the home, that a child will achieve outstanding results. The encouragement of parents and teachers together set a positive tone for the child's learning environment and progress.

As a parent you help your child learn every day. This book can assist with the learning processes needed for development of mathematics.

Enjoy the journey!

Numbers 1 to 10

1. Write the numerals for these.

a. six ☐ b. eight ☐

c. four ☐ d. nine ☐

e. three ☐ f. ten ☐

2. Fill in the missing numbers.

a.

	6		8	9	10

b.

7		5	4		

3. Write the numbers before and after these.

a. ☐ 6 ☐

b. ☐ 9 ☐

4. Count the number.

 ☐

5. Write the next two numbers.

a. 3 ☐ ☐   b. 8 ☐ ☐

Numbers 1 to 20

6. Match the numbers to the group with that many in it.

a. fifteen

b. eleven

c. sixteen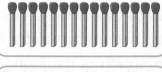

d. fourteen

7. Write the number for these.

a. seventeen ☐   b. twelve ☐

c. nineteen ☐   d. thirteen ☐

e. sixteen ☐   f. twenty ☐

8. Count the number in each group.

a. ☐

b. ☐

9. Fill in the missing numbers

a.

13	14		16		18		20

b.

19	18			15	14		12

10. How many more needed to total 20.

a. 9 ☐   b. 13 ☐   c. 16 ☐

New Syllabus Mentals and Extension 1, Stage On

Numbers to 20

1. Fill in the missing numbers.

8	9			12			15

2. Write the numbers before and after these.

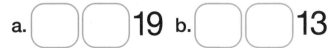

a. ◯ ◯ **17** ◯ ◯ ◯

b. ◯ **12** ◯ ◯ ◯

3. Counting backwards, write the two numbers before these.

a. ◯ ◯ **19**   b. ◯ ◯ **13**

c. ◯ ◯ **15**   d. ◯ ◯ **8**

4. Write these numbers.

a. seven ◯   b. eighteen ◯

c. eleven ◯   d. fourteen ◯

5. How many in each group?

◯   ◯

6. Write each number in words.

a. 17 _____

b. 8 _____

c. 13 _____

7. How many more needed to make 17.

a. 9 ◯   b. 13 ◯   c. 16 ◯

Numbers Zero to 30

8. Write the numeral.

a. twenty-five ◯   b. thirty ◯

c. twenty-one ◯   d. twenty ◯

e. twenty-seven ◯   f. eleven ◯

g. twenty-nine ◯   h. twelve ◯

9. Count the tens and ones.

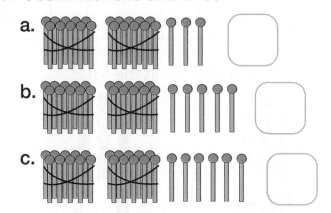

a. ◯

b. ◯

c. ◯

10. Count the number in each group.

a. ◯

b. ◯

11. Fill in the number in each group.

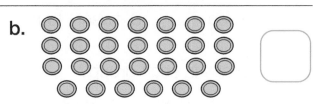

a. | 12 | | | 18 | 20 | |

b. | 20 | | 18 | | | 15 |

12. How many fish in each bowl?

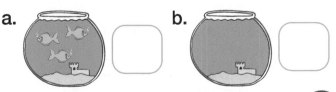

a. ◯   b. ◯

Numbers Zero 0 to 30

1. Write these numbers in words.

a. 0 _____ b. 6 _____

c. 21 _____

d. 27 _____

2. Fill in the missing numbers.

a. | 7 | 8 | | | 11 | | 13 |

b. | 19 | | | 22 | | 24 | 25 |

3. Add the blocks. Fill in the totals.

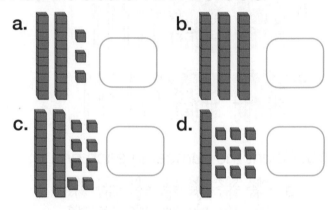

a. ☐ b. ☐

c. ☐ d. ☐

4. Write these as numbers.

a. twenty-two ☐ b. nineteen ☐

c. seventeen ☐ d. twenty-four ☐

5. How many in each group?

a. ☐

b. ☐

6. Write the next two numbers.

a. 24 ☐ ☐ b. 28 ☐ ☐

Extension

7. Draw a line to match numbers in words to written numbers.

(twenty-five) (nineteen) (eight)

19   22   25   29   8   30

(twenty-nine) (thirty) (twenty-two)

8. Compare numbers and colour the correct cards.

a.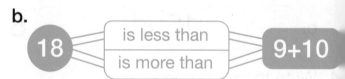
27 — is equal to / is not equal to — 16+9

b.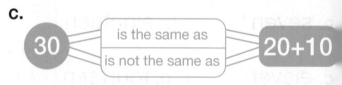
18 — is less than / is more than — 9+10

c.
30 — is the same as / is not the same as — 20+10

9. Write two numbers before these.

a. ☐ ☐ 27 b. ☐ ☐ 12

c. ☐ ☐ 15 d. ☐ ☐ 10

10. What number is missing in this pattern?

12, 14, 18, 20, 22 ☐

11. Write the number shown by the paddle pop sticks.

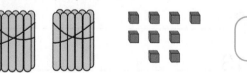

☐

12. Write this number in words.

26 _____

New Syllabus Mentals and Extension 1, Stage One

Numbers 10 to 100

1. There are ten paddle pop sticks in each bundle. Write the number of 10s.

a.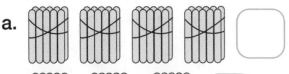

b.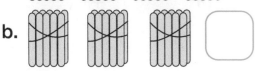

2. Write the words as numbers.

a. forty ☐   b. sixty ☐

c. ninety ☐   d. seventy ☐

e. eighty ☐   f. thirty ☐

g. twenty ☐   h. fifty ☐

3. Count the blocks. Write how many.

a.    b.

4. What rule is used in this pattern? Colour your choice.

| 20 | 30 | 40 | 50 | 60 | 70 | 80 |

(+10)   (-10)

5. Use your knowledge of ten to make speed signs.

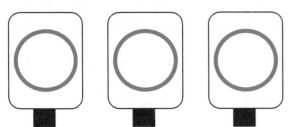

6. How many tens?

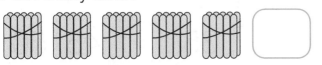

Extension

7. Join each number to where it fits on the number line.

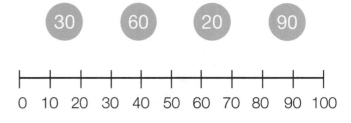

(30)   (60)   (20)   (90)

0 10 20 30 40 50 60 70 80 90 100

8. Fill in the missing numbers in each pattern.

a.		10	20			50		70
b.	30	40			70	80		100

9. Write the numbers ten before and ten after these.

a. ☐ 40 ☐   b. ☐ 80 ☐

c. ☐ 50 ☐   d. ☐ 70 ☐

10. How many groups of ten paddle pop sticks here.

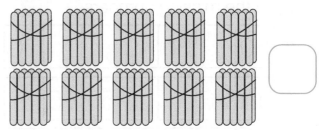 ☐

11. Counting by tens write the next two numbers.

a. 47 ☐ ☐   b. 62 ☐ ☐

c. 19 ☐ ☐   d. 8 ☐ ☐

12. Compare the numbers. Colour the card.

(40)   is the same as / is not the same as   (70)

Counting by Tens

1. Order the numbers - the lowest first.

a.

40 60
30 50 80
70

_____
_____
_____
_____
_____
_____

b.

25 45
55 5 35
15

_____
_____
_____
_____
_____
_____

2. Join each number to its number line.

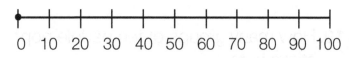

0 10 20 30 40 50 60 70 80 90 100

3. Write the missing numbers.

a.

10		30	40			70

b.

15	25		45	55	65	

c.

27	37	47		67		87

4. How much money?

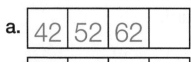

cents

5. What comes next? Look closely.

a.

42	52	62	

b.

81	71	61	

Counting by Fives

6. Write the number of fingers.

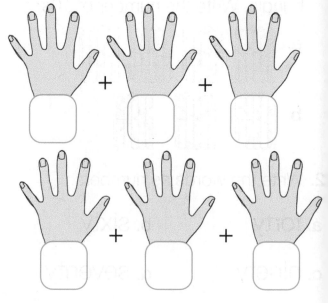

7. Place the numbers along the line. Count as you go.

5

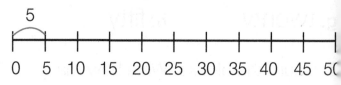

0 5 10 15 20 25 30 35 40 45 50

8. Count in fives to find each total.

a.  = ☐ cents

b. = ☐ cents

9. Write the missing numbers.

a.

5	10		20	25		35

b.

95	90	85	80		70	

10. Write the next number counting by 5s.

a. 25 ☐   b. 50 ☐

11. Write the missing number counting by 5s.

☐ 35, ☐ 45, 50

New Syllabus Mentals and Extension 1, Stage On

Counting by Twos

1. Count the number in each group.

a. 

b. 

c. 

d. 

e. 

2. Write the numbers above in order.

3. Write the next number counting by 2s.

◯ 4, 6, ◯ 10 ◯

4. Count the number in each group.

a. 

b. 

c. 

d. 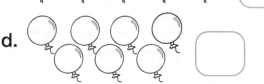

5. Write the numbers above in order.

6. Write the next even and odd number.

a. | 4 | |
   |---|---|

b. | 4 | |
   |---|---|

Counting by Twos, Fives and Tens

7. Complete each number pattern then complete the rule.

a.
2	4		8		12

Counting forwards by _____

b.
10	15			25	30	

Counting forwards by _____

c.
20			16	14		10

Counting backwards by _____

d.
30			50	60		80

Counting backwards by _____

8. Write the missing numbers.

a. 2, 4, ___, 8, ___, 12

b. 10, 20, ___, 40, 50, ___

c. 85, ___, 75, 70, ___, ___

9. Write one coin equal in value to each set.

a.  = _____

b.  = _____

10. Write the missing number counting by 5s.

a. ◯ 55 ◯   b. ◯ 70 ◯

Counting by Twos, Fives and Tens

1. Write the missing numbers.

a. 2, ☐ 6, 8, ☐ 12, ☐

b. 20, 30, ☐ 50, ☐ 70

c. 5, 10, ☐ 20, 25 ☐

2. Colour the odd numbers to count by 2s.

| 1 | 2 | 3 | 4 | 5 | 6 | 7 | 8 | 9 |

3. Write the odd numbers counting by 2s.

| | | | | |

4. Draw a line to match a number to its word.

4

14

40

20

50

65

twenty

forty

fifty

fourteen

sixty-five

four

5. Add these. Count on by 5s.

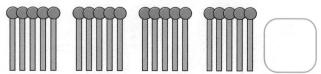 ☐

6. Add these. Count on by 10s.

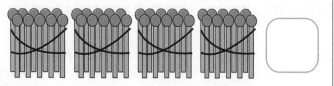 ☐

Counting by Twos, Fives and Tens

7. Fill in the missing numbers.

1		3		5		7		9	
11	12	13	14		16	17	18	19	
21	22	23	24		26	27	28	29	
31	32	33	34		36	37	38	39	

8. Write the number for each name.

a. sixty ☐ b. eighty ☐

c. forty ☐ d. thirty ☐

9. Write the tens and ones in each group.

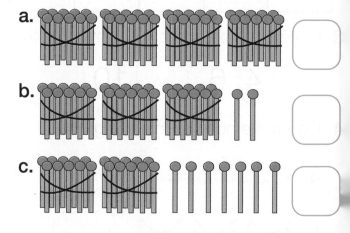

a. ☐

b. ☐

c. ☐

10. Write the missing numbers.

a.

| 2 | | 6 | 8 | | 12 |

b.

| 10 | | 30 | | | 60 |

11. Draw a line from each number to where it fits on the number line.

 12   4   18   10

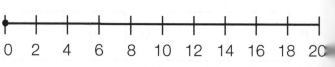

0 2 4 6 8 10 12 14 16 18 20

New Syllabus Mentals and Extension 1, Stage One

Counting by Tens, Fives and Tens

1. Complete each number pattern.

a.  10 20 ◯ ◯ ◯

b. 25 ☐ 35 40 ☐

c. 90 80 ⬠ ⬠ ⬠

2. Count by 10 to add the coins.

How much? ☐ cents

3. Skip count by 5s

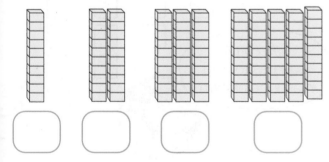

What is the total number of dots on the dice faces? ☐

4. Now count the blocks of ten. Write a number.

☐ ☐ ☐ ☐

5. Write the missing number in each row.

a. | 6 | 8 | 10 | 14 | 16 | ☐ |

b. | 50 | 55 | 65 | 70 | 75 | 80 | ☐ |

c. | 24 | 22 | 20 | 16 | 14 | 12 | ☐ |

d. | 100 | 90 | 80 | 60 | 50 | 40 | ☐ |

Extension

6. What number is missing from this pattern.

| 37 | 52 | 62 | 67 | 72 | 77 | ☐ |

7. How many toes on the feet of 6 children? ☐

8. What number am I?

I am an odd number and 6 less than 22+9. ☐

9. Write the new price for the cricket bat after it has been discounted by $5. $ ☐

$87

10. Write two numbers 5 less and two numbers 5 more than these.

a. ☐ ☐ **22** ☐ ☐

b. ☐ ☐ **64** ☐ ☐

11. What is the value of these coins added together? ☐ cents

12. Fill in the missing numbers when counting backwards by twos.

| 31 | | 27 | 25 | | | 19 |

13. How many 5 cent coins in 50 cents? ☐

14. How many 10 cent coins in one dollar? ☐

Simple Patterns

1. Colour the shapes that do not belong.

a.

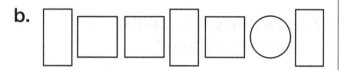

b.

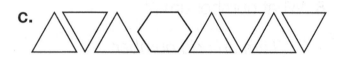

c.

2. Continue each pattern.

a.

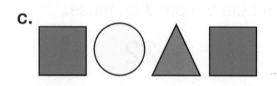 ....

b.

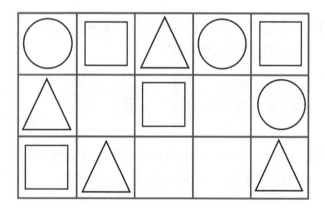 ....

c.

....

3. Add the missing shapes.

4. Add the missing shapes.

a.

5	10	15			

b.

0	2	4	6		

More Patterns and Numbers

5. Fill in the missing numbers on the number chart.

1	2		4	5
6		8	9	10
	12	13		
16	17		19	20
	22		24	

6. Write the numbers counting by twos from zero to twelve.

7. Add more squares to complete this pattern.

Draw small squares to help make the pattern.

8. How many square did you add to complete the pattern?

9. Copy this pattern under the shapes.

   New Syllabus Mentals and Extension 1, Stage On

Ordinal Numbers

1. Colour the fourth ball.

2. Colour the second fish.

3. Colour the fifth cake.

4. Match each rosette to its ordinal name.

a.  1st

b. 4th

c. 3rd

fourth

ninth

first

third

tenth

5. Write these ordinal numbers.

a. sixth ☐ **b.** fiftieth ☐

c. eighth ☐ **d.** second ☐

e. twenty-first ☐ **f.** fifth ☐

g. thirtieth ☐ **h.** third ☐

. Write the full date for today.

_____

Ordinal Number

7. Fill in the missing ordinal numbers.

1st	2nd		4th		6th

8. Match these ordinal numbers to their names.

31st   twenty-third

20th   twenty-seventh

23rd   thirty-first

27th   twentieth

9. Colour the dates on the calendar.

9th, 12th, eighth, 17th, 28th, 31st

CALENDAR						
	1st	2nd	3rd	4th	5th	6th
7th	8th	9th	10th	11th	12th	13th
14th	15th	16th	17th	18th	19th	20th
21st	22nd	23rd	24th	25th	26th	27th
28th	29th	30th	31st			

10.a. Name the sixth letter of the alphabet. ☐

b. Name the tenth letter of the alphabet. ☐

11. Write the position of three letters in the alphabet.

a. Letter 'c' ☐ **b.** Letter 'f' ☐

c. Letter 'g' ☐

Introducing Place Value

1. Fill in the place value cards for the number of matches and blocks.

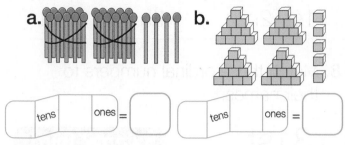

a. tens ones =

b. tens ones =

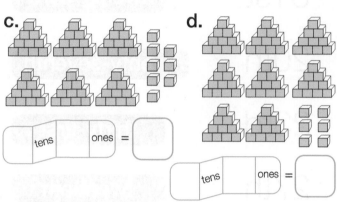

c. tens ones =

d. tens ones =

2. What numbers are shown on each abacus?

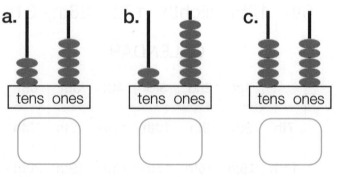

a. tens ones

b. tens ones

c. tens ones

3. Write the whole number on each place card.

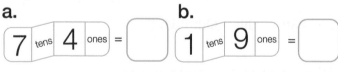

a. 7 tens 4 ones =

b. 1 tens 9 ones =

c. 8 tens 5 ones =

d. 6 tens 3 ones =

4. Write these numbers.

a. sixty-eight

b. fifty-seven

5. Tick the place value of tens in 46.

Place value is 4 tens or 6 tens

Continuing Place Value

6. Write the whole number shown on the place value card.

a. 37
  tens ones =

b. 45
  tens ones =

c. 29
  tens ones =

d. 86
  tens ones =

7. Write the number shown on each abacus

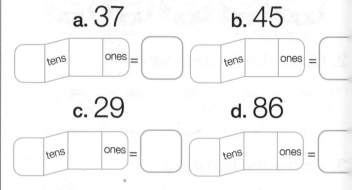

a. tens ones

b. tens ones

c. tens one

8. Show the number of paddle pop sticks on each abacus.

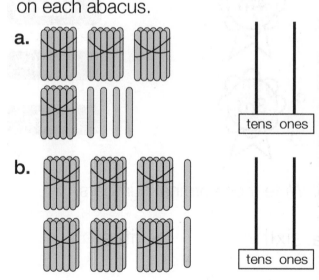

a. tens ones

b. tens ones

9. Write the whole numbers.

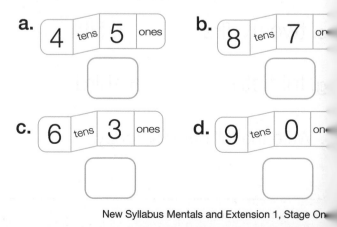

a. 4 tens 5 ones

b. 8 tens 7 on

c. 6 tens 3 ones

d. 9 tens 0 on

Place Value

. Write the number showing on each abacus.

a.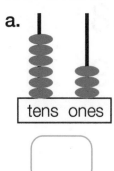

b.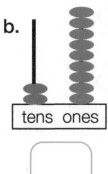

. Draw beads on the abacus to show each number.

a. **36**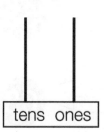

b. **54**

What numbers are shown on the place value cards?

a.  7 tens 3 ones =

b.  5 tens 8 ones =

c.  6 tens 4 ones =

d.  9 tens 7 ones =

Show the value of the blocks on the place value card.

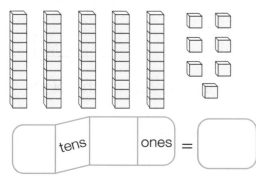

tens   ones =

Ordinal Number

5. Write the whole number shown on the place value card.

a. 6 tens 8 ones

b. 3 tens 5 ones

c. 4 tens 9 ones

d. 4 tens 1 ones

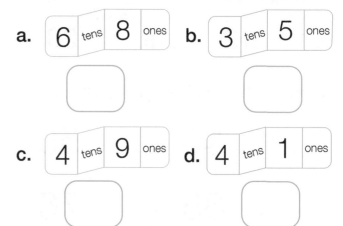

6. Write these numbers on the place value cards.

a. 37

b. 45

c. 29

d. 86

e. 77

f. 96

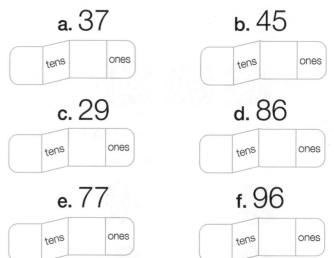

7. Write the number shown on each abacus.

a.

b.

c.

d.

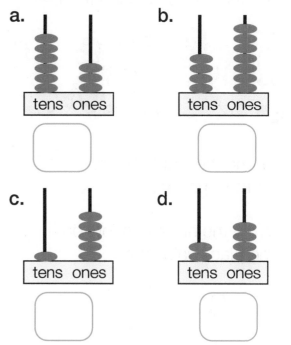

15

Extension – Numbers, Patterns, Place Value

1. Write the numbers before and after these.

a. ( ) 12 ( )   b. ( ) 20 ( )

3. Write the number five less than these.

a. ( ) 10   b. ( ) 50

c. ( ) 35   d. ( ) 76

5. Complete each number pattern.

a. 6 8 10 ( ) ( )

b. 15 20 25 [ ] [ ]

7. Continue the pattern by adding the two coloured shapes in each.

a. ▮ ▲ ● ▮ ....

b. ● ▮ ▮ ● ....

9. Tick the runner coming third.

11. Name the eighth letter of the alphabet. ( )

13. Write the number show on the place value card.

8 |tens| 3 |ones| = ( )

2. Write the number two more than these.

a. 27 ( )   b. 38 ( )

c. 51 ( )   d. 89 ( )

4. Write 61 in words.

_____

6. Compare numbers then colour the correct card.

a. 27 — is less than / is more than — 53

b. 86 — is less than / is more than — 68

8. Fill in the missing numbers.

	10	20		40
50	60		80	

10. Write the ordinal numbers in words.

a. 4th _____   b. 9th _____

12. Write the number on each abacus.

a. [abacus] tens ones ( )   b. [abacus] tens ones ( )

14. Show this number on the place value card.

( ) |tens| ( ) |ones| = 76

New Syllabus Mentals and Extension 1, Stage On

Simple Addition

1. Fill in the number sentences.

a.

[ ] and [ ] make [ ]

b.

[ ] and [ ] and [ ] make [ ]

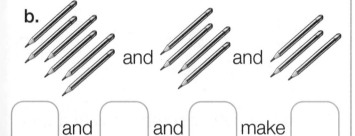

2. Count the objects. Write a complete number sentence.

a.

[ ] + [ ] = [ ]

b.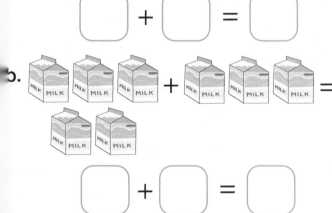

[ ] + [ ] = [ ]

3. Add these with numbers only.

a. 7+3 = [ ]   **b.** 10 +9 = [ ]

c. 10+6 = [ ]   **d.** 2+5 = [ ]

Addition

4. Add each group of fruit.
Write the number sentence.

a.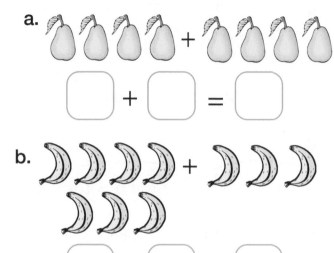

[ ] + [ ] = [ ]

b.

[ ] + [ ] = [ ]

5. Complete these number sentences.

a. 4 + 6 = [ ]

b. 3 + 7 = [ ]

c. 2 + 8 = [ ]

6. Add the dots. Write their totals.

a. 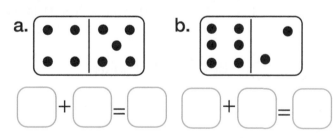   **b.**

[ ] + [ ] = [ ]   [ ] + [ ] = [ ]

7. Add the number in the centre to each one in the next circle. Write the total.

Number Line Additions

1. Use the number line to add.
Fill in the number sentences.

a.

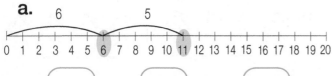

⬜ and ⬜ make ⬜

b.

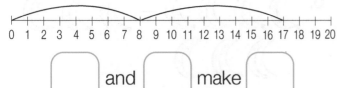

⬜ and ⬜ make ⬜

c.

⬜ and ⬜ and ⬜ make ⬜

2. Show these additions on the number line.

a. [8] and [6] make ⬜

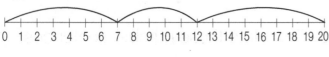

b. [5] and [11] make ⬜

3. Add these numbers.

a. 7 and 4 and 5 make ⬜

b. 3 and 6 and 8 make ⬜

c. 6 and 4 and 9 make ⬜

Addition with Concrete Materia[l]

4. Add the group. Match it to its total.

a.
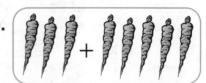 [7]

b.
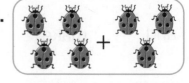 [9]

c.
 [8]

d.
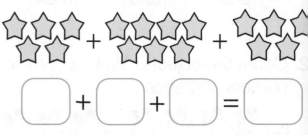 [10]

5. Write a number sentence with a total.

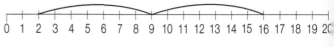

⬜ + ⬜ + ⬜ = ⬜

6. Use the number lines to add three numbers. Fill in the number sentences

a.

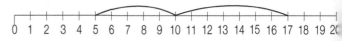

⬜ + ⬜ + ⬜ = ⬜

b.

⬜ + ⬜ + ⬜ = ⬜

c.

⬜ + ⬜ + ⬜ = ⬜

Addition Combinations 5 and 10

1. Complete the addition combinations to 5.

5	+	0	=	5
4	+		=	5
3	+		=	5
2	+		=	5
1	+		=	5
0	+		=	5

2. Fill in the missing numbers for the addition of combinations for 10.

0	+	10	=	10
1	+		=	10
2	+		=	10
3	+	7	=	
4	+		=	10
5	+		=	10
6	+	4	=	
7	+		=	10
8	+		=	10
9	+	1	=	
10	+		=	10

3. Add the numbers around the outside of the circle to the centre ten.

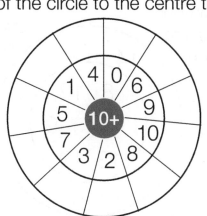

Addition Combination Pattern

4. Complete the sentences for 7 and 8.

a.

0	+	7	=	7
1	+	6	=	
2	+	5	=	
3	+	4	=	
4	+	3	=	
5	+	2	=	
6	+	1	=	
7	+	0	=	

b.

0	+	8	=	8
1	+	7	=	
2	+	6	=	
3	+	5	=	
4	+	4	=	
5	+	3	=	
6	+	2	=	
7	+	1	=	
8	+	0	=	

5. Add these three numbers. Look for combinations.

a. $7 + 3 + 3 =$ ⬚

b. $4 + 6 + 9 =$ ⬚

c. $5 + 5 + 7 =$ ⬚

d. $10 + 6 + 2 =$ ⬚

6. Try these additions. Remember combinations.

a. $8 + 4 + 6 =$ ⬚

b. $9 + 2 + 8 =$ ⬚

c. $7 + 6 + 3 =$ ⬚

d. $10 + 4 + 2 =$ ⬚

Vertical Addition and Numbers

1. Add circles to the tens frame to complete each addition.

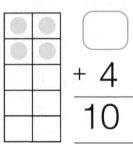

a. + 4 / 10

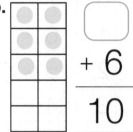

b. + 6 / 10

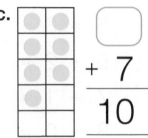

c. + 7 / 10

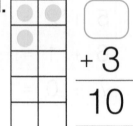

d. + 3 / 10

2. Find the missing number and add the triangles to each frame.

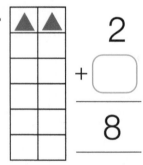

a. 2 / + ☐ / 8

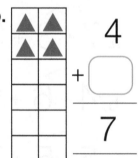

b. 4 / + ☐ / 7

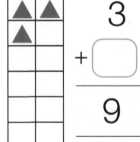

c. 3 / + ☐ / 9

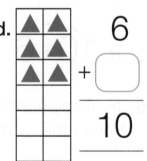

d. 6 / + ☐ / 10

3. Add circles and numbers to each addition.

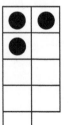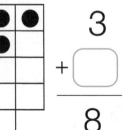

a. 3 / + ☐ / 8

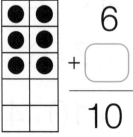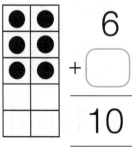

b. 6 / + ☐ / 10

Vertical Additions to 20

4. Add these numbers vertically.

a. 6
  +2
____

b. 5
  +6
____

c. 7
  +1
____

d. 8
  +5
____

5. Add these numbers vertically.

a. 7
  +9
____

b. 8
  +9
____

c. 6
  +8
____

d. 9
  +9
____

6. Add these numbers vertically.

a. 6
   2
  +3
____

b. 8
   3
  +7
____

c. 10
   7
  +1
____

d. 7
   6
  +5
____

e. 8
   4
  +3
____

f. 12
   6
  +2
____

7. Add the number in the middle to each number in the next circle. Finish the outside circle.

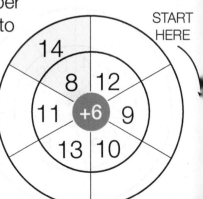

START HERE

14

8 12

11 +6 9

13 10

New Syllabus Mentals and Extension 1, Stage One

Adding Two-Digit Numbers to 100

1. Add these blocks.

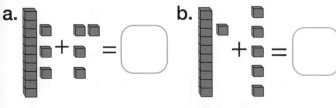

a. [ ] + [ ] = ( ) b. [ ] + [ ] = ( )

c. [ ] + [ ] = ( ) d. [ ] + [ ] = ( )

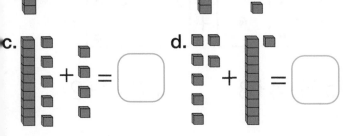

2. Remember place value, tens and ones. Add these numbers in frames.

a.
Tens	Ones
1	3
+	6

b.
Tens	Ones
	6
+ 1	1

c.
Tens	Ones
1	5
+	2

d.
Tens	Ones
1	2
+	8

3. Add these two-digit numbers.

a.
Tens	Ones
3	2
+ 1	4

b.
Tens	Ones
5	3
+ 2	2

c.
Tens	Ones
4	4
+ 2	5

d.
Tens	Ones
4	2
+ 3	6

e.
Tens	Ones
4	7
+ 3	1

f.
Tens	Ones
6	1
+ 2	8

Vertical Addition

4. Write the sentence in the addition frames, then write totals.

a. $14+13=$ ( )   b. $25+32=$ ( )

+
Tens	Ones

+
Tens	Ones

c. $27+42=$ ( )   d. $38+20=$ ( )

+
Tens	Ones

+
Tens	Ones

5. Add these three-digit numbers.

a.
H	T	O
1	2	4
+ 4	6	3

b.
H	T	O
2	5	6
+ 7	1	3

c.
H	T	O
2	3	6
+ 5	2	3

d.
H	T	O
2	5	4
+ 6	3	4

6. Darcy swam 250 metres on Tuesday and 325 metres on Friday. How many metres did he swim? Fill in the frame.

+
H	T	O

7.

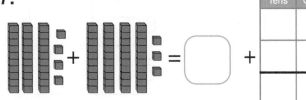

[ ] + [ ] = ( ) +
Tens	Ones

More Addition

1. Show these addition on a number line. Fill in the totals.

a. $7 + 4 + 6 =$ ◯

0 1 2 3 4 5 6 7 8 9 10 11 12 13 14 15 16 17 18 19 20

b. $5 + 3 + 9 =$ ◯

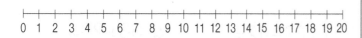

0 1 2 3 4 5 6 7 8 9 10 11 12 13 14 15 16 17 18 19 20

2. Add numbers down the side to the top numbers to complete the table.

+	2	4	5	7	6
a. 8					
b. 4					
c. 5					
d. 6					

3. What is the addition or take away rule for each pattern. One is done for you.

Pattern	Rule
2, 4, 6, 8, 10	+2
a. 10, 20, 30, 40, 50	
b. 25, 30, 35, 40, 45	
c. 100, 90, 80, 70, 60	
d. 10, 9, 8, 7, 6, 5	
e. 21, 26, 31, 36, 41	

Extension – Addition

1. 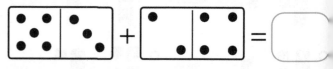 plus = ◯

2. Add the dots - "Counting On."

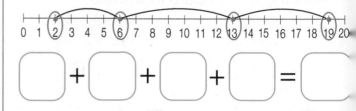 = ◯

3. $6+4+3=$ ◯ **4.** $8+4+2=$ ◯

5. Fill in the number sentence shown on the number line.

0 1 2 3 4 5 6 7 8 9 10 11 12 13 14 15 16 17 18 19 20

◯ + ◯ + ◯ + ◯ = ◯

6. Fill in the missing numbers.

a. $6+1=$ ◯ **b.** $4+3=$ ◯

7. Fill in the number sentence.

◯ + ◯ + ◯ = ◯

8. Add the numbers in the centre to those around the outside.

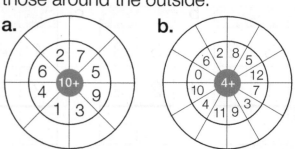

a. centre 10+ with 2 7 5 9 3 1 4 6

b. centre 4+ with 2 8 5 12 7 3 9 11 4 10 0 6

9.a.

Tens	Ones
1	4
+ 3	3

b.

Tens	Ones
2	4
+ 6	3

c.

H	T	O
4	1	5
+ 2	6	3

New Syllabus Mentals and Extension 1, Stage On

Introducing Subtraction

1. Cross off to take away. Fill in the
number sentences.

a.

[ ] take away [ ] leaves [ ]

b.

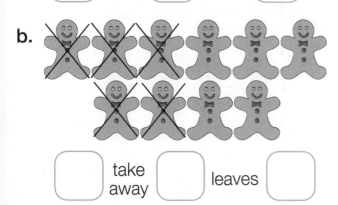

[ ] take away [ ] leaves [ ]

take away, minus, subtract
and - all mean the same.

2. Cross of the number needed
to take away. Count those left.

a. 7 - 3 equals [ ]

b. 9 - 2 equals [ ]

3. Take away the smallest number in
each group.

a. 10-6 = [ ] **b.** 8-2 = [ ]

c. 9-3 = [ ] **d.** 7-4 = [ ]

e. 10-4 = [ ] **f.** 10-5 = [ ]

Cross Off Method – Subtraction

4. Cross off three trees then fill in the
sentence.

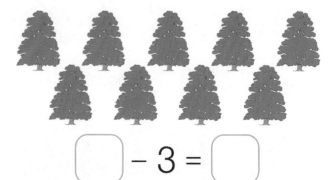

[ ] – 3 = [ ]

5. Cross off 6 balloons then fill in
the sentence.

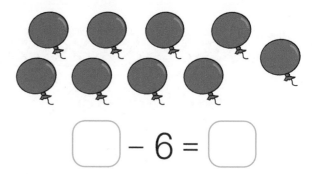

[ ] – 6 = [ ]

6. Count the stars. Cross off those
needed so only 3 are left.

[ ] – [ ] leaves 3

7. Cross off the number of counters
needed so only 5 are left.

[ ] – [ ] leaves 5

8. Cross off the number of counters
needed so only 5 are left.

a. 14-7 = [ ] **b.** 15-9 = [ ]

c. 18-12 = [ ]

Subtraction

1. Write the number sentences.

a.

 take away equals [ ]

b.

[ ] – [ ] = [ ]

c.

[ ] – [ ] = [ ]

2. Complete the sentence then cross off the flowers to match.

$$12 - 5 = \boxed{}$$

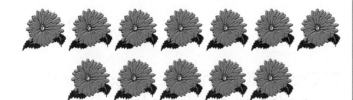

3. Complete these.

a. $8 - 4 = \boxed{}$

b. $9 - 3 = \boxed{}$

c. $10 - 2 = \boxed{}$

d. – = [ ] cents

Subtraction Combinations

4. Fill in the missing numbers in each subtraction combinations.

10	–	0	=	
9	–	1	=	
8	–	2	=	
7	–	3	=	
6	–	4	=	
5	–	5	=	
4	+	6	=	
3	+	7	=	
2	+	8	=	
1	+	9	=	
0	+	10	=	

5. Complete these for 6 and 9.

a.

6	–	0	=	
6	–	1	=	
6	–	2	=	
6	–	3	=	
6	–	4	=	
6	–	5	=	
6	–	6	=	

b.

9	–	0	=	
9	–	1	=	
9	–	2	=	
9	–	3	=	
9	–	4	=	
9	–	5	=	
9	–	6	=	
9	–	7	=	
9	–	8	=	
9	–	9	=	

6. Write the number sentence.

[ ] – [ ] = [ ]

New Syllabus Mentals and Extension 1, Stage On

Find the Difference

1. Find the difference between each group.

a.

$\boxed{} - \boxed{} = \boxed{}$

b.

$\boxed{} - \boxed{} = \boxed{}$

c.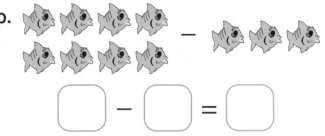

$\boxed{} - \boxed{} = \boxed{}$

d.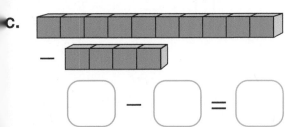

$\boxed{} - \boxed{} = \boxed{}$

2. Count the number and take away the ones crossed off. Write the number left.

a.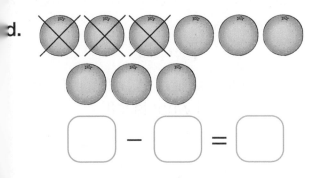

$\boxed{} - 5 = \boxed{}$

b.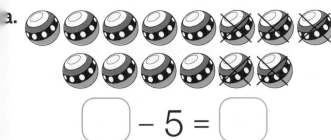

$\boxed{} - 6 = \boxed{}$

Simple Subtraction

3. Count the fruit then take away those crossed off. Write the number sentence.

a.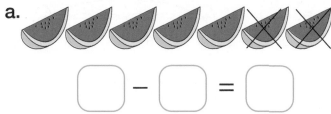

$\boxed{} - \boxed{} = \boxed{}$

b.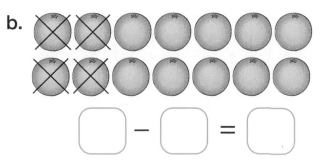

$\boxed{} - \boxed{} = \boxed{}$

4. Complete each sentence.

a.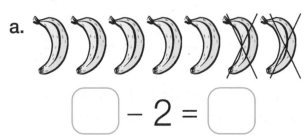

$\boxed{} - 2 = \boxed{}$

b.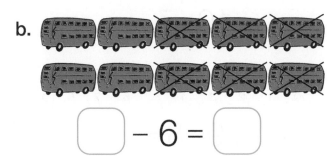

$\boxed{} - 6 = \boxed{}$

c.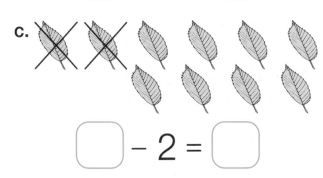

$\boxed{} - 2 = \boxed{}$

5. Try these subtractions.

a. $17 - 4 = \boxed{}$ **b.** $20 - 6 = \boxed{}$

c. $15 - 9 = \boxed{}$ **d.** $19 - 7 = \boxed{}$

Number Line Subtraction

1. Count backwards to take away on the number line. Fill in the sentences.

a.

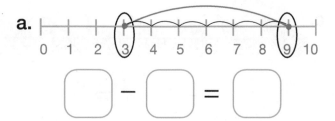

☐ – ☐ = ☐

b.

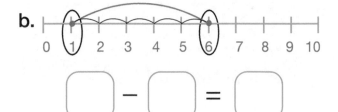

☐ – ☐ = ☐

c.

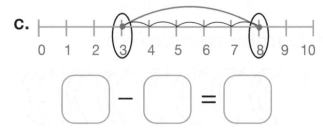

☐ – ☐ = ☐

2. Count backwards to take away on the number line. Fill in the sentences.

a. $10 - 7 =$ ☐

b. $9 - 8 =$ ☐

3. Count backwards on the number lines to find how many are left.

a. $10 - 7 =$ ☐

b. $20 - 17 =$ ☐

Using Number Lines

4. Count backwards on the number lines to find how many are left.

a.

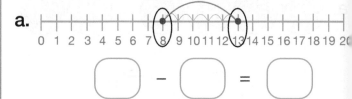

☐ – ☐ = ☐

b.

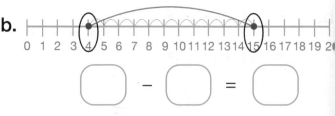

☐ – ☐ = ☐

c.

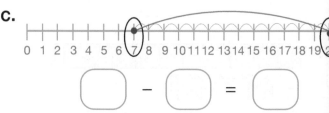

☐ – ☐ = ☐

d.

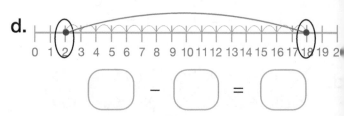

☐ – ☐ = ☐

5. Use the number line to help find the differences and what is left.

a. $18 - 6 =$ ☐ **b.** $14 - 8 =$ ☐

c. $20 - 7 =$ ☐ **d.** $15 - 9 =$ ☐

e. $19 - 12 =$ ☐ **f.** $16 - 7 =$ ☐

6. Take the side number away from the top number. Fill in the squares.

-	12	14	15	17	19	20
a. 4						
b. 7						
c. 6						

New Syllabus Mentals and Extension 1, Stage On

Introducing Vertical Subtraction

1. Cross off the circles in each frame to show the difference.

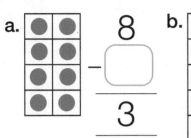

a.   8
   − ( )
   ──
     3

b.   9
   − ( )
   ──
     4

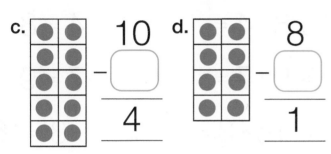

c.   10
   − ( )
   ──
     4

d.   8
   − ( )
   ──
     1

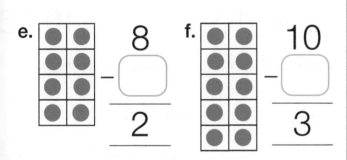

e.   8
   − ( )
   ──
     2

f.   10
   − ( )
   ──
     3

2. Fill in the missing numbers for each subtraction.

a.   12
   − 6
   ──

b.   10
   − 7
   ──

c.   14
   − 7
   ──

d.   18
   − 5
   ──

e.   16
   − 4
   ──

f.   20
   − 9
   ──

3. Try these subtractions.

a. $18 - 4 =$ ( )   b. $17 - 12 =$ ( )

Subtracting Two-Digit Numbers

4. Remember place value, tens and ones, Ones are subtracted first in vertical form.

a.

Tens	Ones
1	8
−	6

b.

Tens	Ones
2	7
−	6

c.

Tens	Ones
3	5
− 1	2

d.

Tens	Ones
4	7
− 1	4

e.

Tens	Ones
6	8
− 2	2

f.

Tens	Ones
7	7
− 4	2

5. Write these subtractions in the frames and find the differences.

a. $28 - 13 =$ ( )   b. $77 - 24 =$ ( )

Tens	Ones
−	

Tens	Ones
−	

6. Complete these three-digit take aways using place value frames.

a.

H	T	O
6	7	8
− 1	2	4

b.

H	T	O
6	9	5
− 4	3	3

7. Mohammad had 76 footy cards. Mum put 22 through the wash. How many left? Fill in the frame.

Tens	Ones
−	

Subtraction Mixed

1. Cross off objects to make each number sentence true.

a.

b.

$12 - 6 = 6$ $9 - 8 = 1$

2. Complete these take away sentences.

a. $8 - 2 = \boxed{}$ b. $9 - 4 = \boxed{}$

c. $10 - 7 = \boxed{}$

3. Try these vertical subtractions.

a. $\begin{array}{r} 9 \\ -4 \\ \hline \end{array}$ b. $\begin{array}{r} 7 \\ -3 \\ \hline \end{array}$ c. $\begin{array}{r} 8 \\ -6 \\ \hline \end{array}$ d. $\begin{array}{r} 10 \\ -1 \\ \hline \end{array}$

4. Start in the centre and take away the number in the next circle. Write the difference in the outside circle.

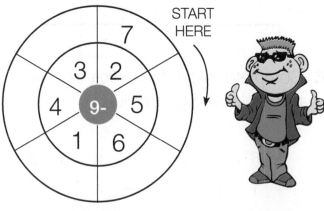

START HERE

5. a.

Tens	Ones
6	8
− 4	3

b.

H	T	O
5	6	7
− 2	4	3

Subtraction and Addition Equations

$6 + 7 = 13$

$13 - 7 = 6$

> Remember additions and subtraction are related. One adds on, the other takes away.

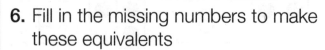

6. Fill in the missing numbers to make these equivalents

a. $8 + 4 = \boxed{}$ $\boxed{} - 4 = 8$

b. $9 + 7 = \boxed{}$ $\boxed{} - 7 = 9$

c. $16 + 3 = \boxed{}$ $\boxed{} - 3 = 16$

d. $12 + 10 = \boxed{}$ $\boxed{} - 10 = 16$

7. Fill in the missing numbers in these.

a. $8 + \boxed{} = 14$ $14 - \boxed{} = 8$

b. $10 + \boxed{} = 19$ $19 - \boxed{} = 10$

c. $22 + \boxed{} = 30$ $30 - \boxed{} = 22$

8. Colour the correct equivalent card for each problem.

a. $\begin{array}{r} 3 \\ +9 \end{array}$ [is equal to / not equal to] $\begin{array}{r} 20 \\ -8 \end{array}$

b. $\begin{array}{r} 7 \\ +9 \end{array}$ [is equal to / not equal to] $\begin{array}{r} 18 \\ -3 \end{array}$

c. $\begin{array}{r} 16 \\ -7 \end{array}$ [is equal to / not equal to] $\begin{array}{r} 11 \\ +6 \end{array}$

d. $\begin{array}{r} 20 \\ -11 \end{array}$ [is equal to / not equal to] $\begin{array}{r} 4 \\ +5 \end{array}$

9. Take the number from the side away from those on the top row.

-	12	18	15	20	25	28
a. 4						
b. 8						
c. 5						

Extension - Subtraction

1. take away leaves ⬜

2. 10 minus 7 = ⬜

3. Fill in the number sentence when some stars are crossed off.

⬜ − ⬜ leaves ⬜

4. Write the number sentence for the block's problem.

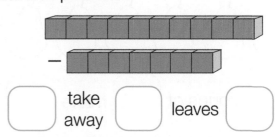

⬜ take away ⬜ leaves ⬜

5. Complete these subtractions.

a. $9 - 4 =$ ⬜   b. $16 - 7 =$ ⬜

c. $26 - 11 =$ ⬜   d. $30 - 19 =$ ⬜

6. Complete these subtractions.

a. $19 -$ ⬜ $= 12$ b. $23 -$ ⬜ $= 11$

c. $30 -$ ⬜ $= 7$ d. $18 -$ ⬜ $= 5$

7. Fill in the subtraction sentence shown on the number line.

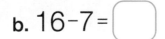

0 1 2 3 4 5 6 7 8 9 10 11 12 13 14 15 16 17 18 19 20

⬜ − ⬜ = ⬜

8. Show this subtraction on the number line.

$7 - 5 =$ ⬜

0 1 2 3 4 5 6 7 8 9 10

9. Cross off triangles in each frame then complete the vertical subtraction.

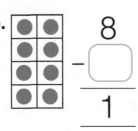

a. 10 − ⬜ = 4   b. 8 − ⬜ = 1

10. Show each subtraction in the vertical frames.

a. $26 - 14 =$ ⬜   b. $425 - 111 =$ ⬜

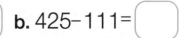

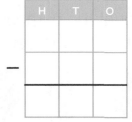

Tens	Ones
−	

H	T	O
−		

11. Fill in the missing numbers in the magic squares.

a.

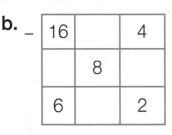

−	19		12
		3	
	11		7

b.

−	16		4
		8	
	6		2

12. Take numbers from the top away from those down the side.

−	6	2	25	3	14
a. 28					
b. 37					

Multiplication – Equal Groups

1. Colour the pears to make two equal groups.

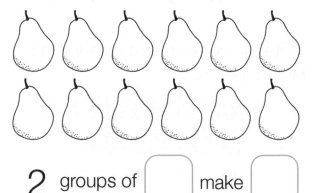

2 groups of ☐ make ☐

2. Count the groups. Write the numbers.

a.

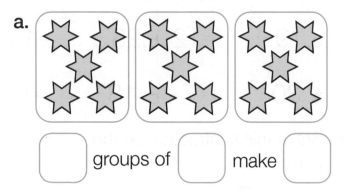

☐ groups of ☐ make ☐

b.

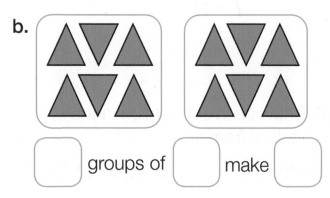

☐ groups of ☐ make ☐

3. Count the number in each row. Fill in the number sentence.

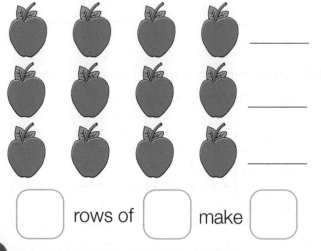

_____

_____

_____

☐ rows of ☐ make ☐

Groups and Rows

4. Write the number sentences.

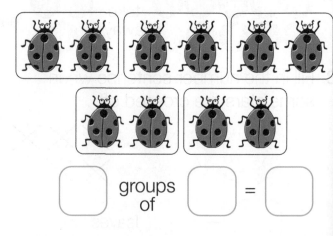

☐ groups of ☐ = ☐

5. Count the number in each row.

a.

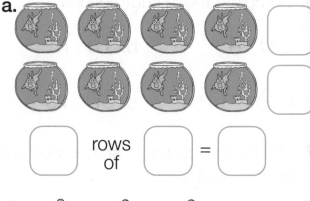

☐ rows of ☐ = ☐

b.

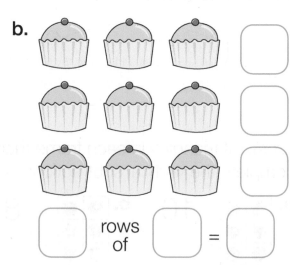

☐ rows of ☐ = ☐

6. Add rows of shapes to match each sentence.

a. ⬤ ⬤ ⬤   b. ▲ ▲ ▲ ▲

2 rows of 3   3 rows of 4

New Syllabus Mentals and Extension 1, Stage On

Groups

1. Colour the balloons to make four equal groups.

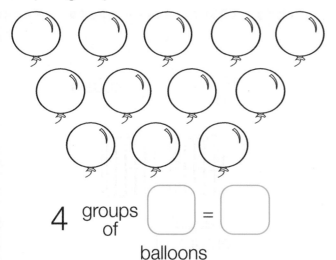

4 groups of ☐ = ☐ balloons

2. Draw triangles to make three equal groups of two. Fill in the number sentence.

3 equal groups of 2 = ☐

3. Colour the mittens to make pairs.

4. How many pairs of mittens? ☐

Groups and Rows

5. Fill in the sentences for these groups.

a.

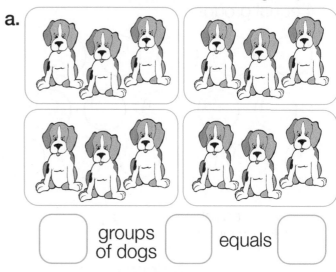

☐ groups of dogs ☐ equals ☐

b.

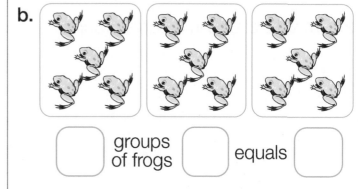

☐ groups of frogs ☐ equals ☐

6. Count these rows.

a.

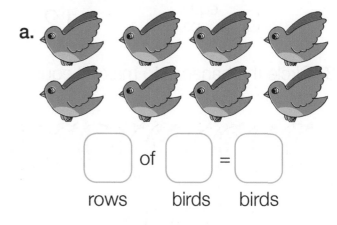

☐ of ☐ = ☐
rows   birds   birds

b.

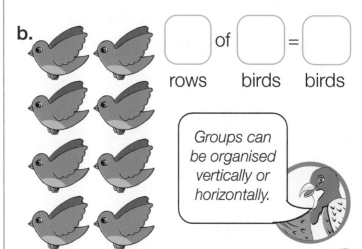

☐ of ☐ = ☐
rows   birds   birds

Groups can be organised vertically or horizontally.

Groups and Sharing

1. Colour the balloons to make 4 equal groups.

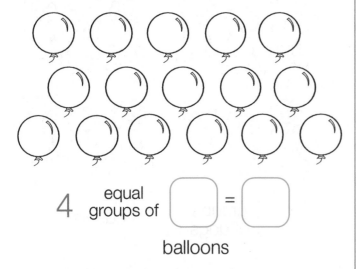

4 equal groups of ☐ = ☐
balloons

2. Draw 12 circles in 3 equal groups.

3 equal groups of ☐ = 12

3. Circle the bananas to make 3 equal groups of 3.

3 equal groups of 3 = ☐

4. Colour the icing on the cakes to make 2 groups of 5.

2 groups of ☐ = ☐

Equal Groups

5. Fill in the missing numbers for these equal groups.

a.

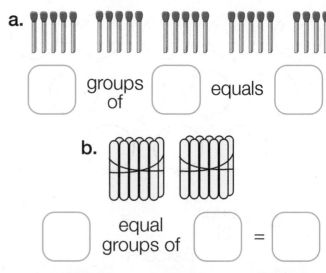

☐ groups of ☐ equals ☐

b.

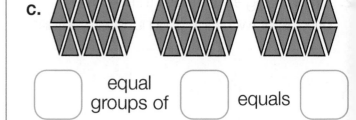

☐ equal groups of ☐ = ☐

c.

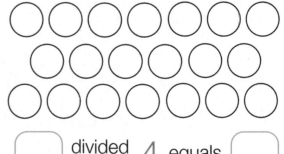

☐ equal groups of ☐ equals ☐

6. a. How many equal groups of 4 can be made from 12? ☐

b. How many equal groups of 6 can be made from 12? ☐

c. How many equal groups of 5 can be made from 20? ☐

7. Divide the counters into 4 equal groups using four different colours.

☐ divided by 4 equals ☐

8.a. How many groups of 7 in 14? ☐   **b.** How many groups of 5 in 25? ☐

More Groups and Rows

1. Count how many in each row.

a.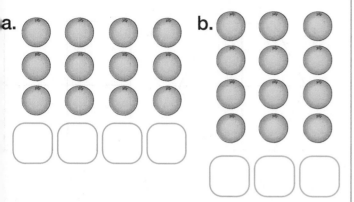

b.

2. True or false: **4** rows of **3** has the same total as **3** rows of **4**. Tick.

True ☐ or False ☐

3. Fill in the numbers for these.

a.

= ☐

= ☐

☐ rows of ☐ = ☐

b.

☐ rows of ☐ = ☐

4. Multiply the centre number with the others.

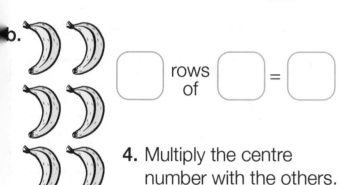

Extension Multiplication and Division

1. Colour the counters to make 3 equal groups.

2. How many in each group? ☐

3. How many pairs of shoes?

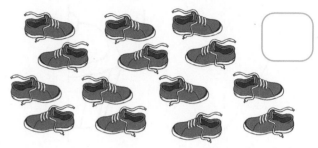 ☐

4. How many groups of 4 here?

 ☐

5. How many equal groups of three can be made with 12 counters? ☐

6. Fill in the number sentence for the oranges.

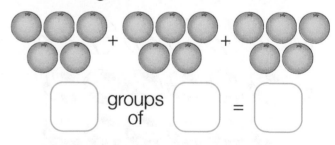

☐ groups of ☐ = ☐

7. Tick Yes or No.
Do these arrays have the same total?

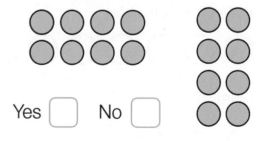

Yes ☐   No ☐

8. Three groups of six is equal to ☐

33

Fractions - Half

1. Colour half of each shape.

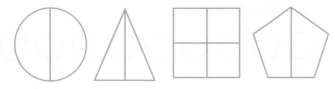

2. Draw the other half of these shapes or objects.

a.    **b.**

c.    **d.**

3. Colour half of each group.

a.

b.

c.

4. Colour half of each group then write how many in a half.

a.

Half of ☐ = ☐

b.

Half of ☐ = ☐

Fraction - Quarter

5. Colour a quarter of each shape.

a. 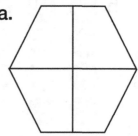   **b.**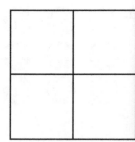

c. 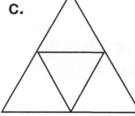   **d.**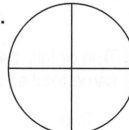

6. How many in a quarter of each group?

a.

b.

7. Colour three quarters of each shape.

a. 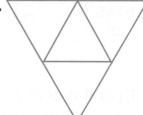   **b.**

c. 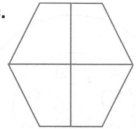   **d.**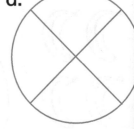

e.

New Syllabus Mentals and Extension 1, Stage On

Fractions

1. Colour a quarter of each object.

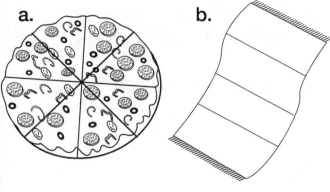

a. b.

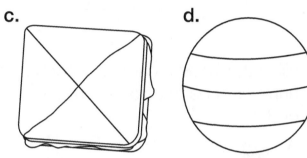

c. d.

2. Colour $\frac{1}{2}$ of each shape.

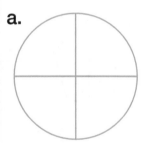

a. b.

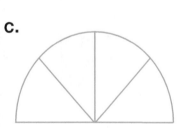
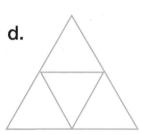

c. d.

3. Colour **one quarter** of this group.

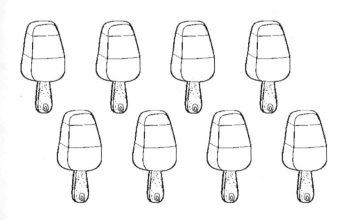

Fractions

4. Colour $\frac{3}{4}$ of these shapes.

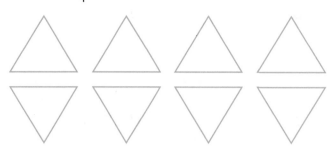

5. Tick the shapes that are a quarter coloured.

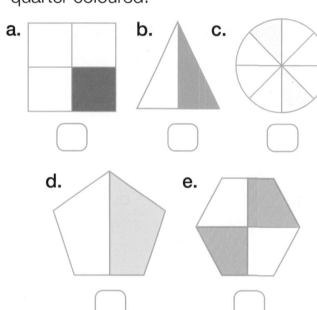

a. b. c.

d. e.

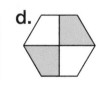

6. Colour the correct name card for the coloured part of each shape.

a. b. c. d.

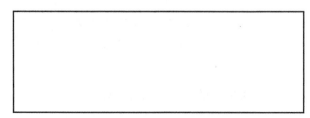

half	half	half	half
quarter	quarter	quarter	quarter
3 quarters	3 quarters	3 quarters	3 quarters

7. Divide this shape into 4 equal parts. Colour one quarter.

Fractions

1. Write how many parts in each shape.

a.
parts

b.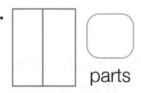
parts

c.
parts

d.
parts

2. Colour **half** of these shapes.

a.

b.

c.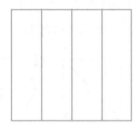

d.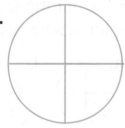

3. Colour a **quarter** of each shape.

a.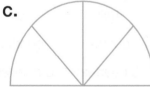

b.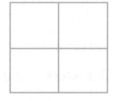

c.

d.

4. Colour a **quarter** of the triangles.

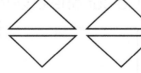

5. How many did you colour?

Fractions – Half, Quarter, 3/4 Quarters

6. Colour **half** the number in each group.

a.

b.

c.

7. Fill in the fraction card to describe the number of parts coloured 1/2, 1/4 or 3/4.

a.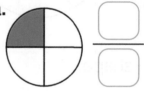

b.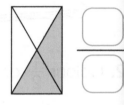

c.

d.

e.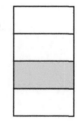

f.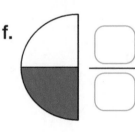

8. Colour the fraction for each group.

a. $\frac{1}{2}$

b. $\frac{1}{4}$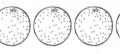

c. $\frac{3}{4}$

New Syllabus Mentals and Extension 1, Stage On

Fractions

1. What fraction of each group is coloured? $\frac{1}{2}$, $\frac{1}{4}$ or $\frac{3}{4}$

a.

b.

c.

2. Draw the other half of each shape then divide it into 4 parts. Colour 3/4.

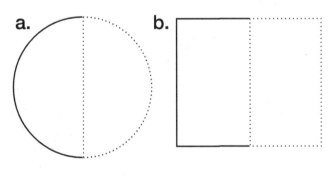

a.   **b.**

c.

3. Write how many for each fraction.

a. Half of 10 = ☐   **b.** Quarter of 12 = ☐

c. Three quarters of 16 = ☐

d. Quarter of 8 = ☐   **e.** Half of 30 = ☐

Extension - Fraction

1. What part of the circle is coloured?
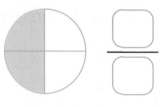
$\frac{\boxed{}}{\boxed{}}$

2. How much pizza is gone?

$\frac{\boxed{}}{\boxed{}}$

3. How many in half of this group?
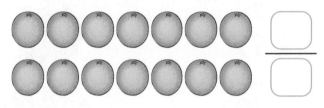
$\frac{\boxed{}}{\boxed{}}$

4. Colour the shapes divided into quarters.

5. Colour three quarters of the rectangle.

6. How many in a quarter of this group?

☐

7. Colour the fraction for each group.

a. $\frac{1}{2}$

b. $\frac{1}{4}$

8. a. How many in a quarter of 8? ☐

b. How many in a half of 18? ☐

c. How many in $\frac{3}{4}$ of 20? ☐

Money – Australian Coins
OPTIONAL EXTENSION

1. Match each coin face to its reverse side picture.

2. Colour the coins **less** than one dollar.

Naming and Working with Coins
OPTIONAL EXTENSION

3. Match the coins to their names.

a.

twenty cents

b.

ten cents

c.

two dollars

d.

fifty cents

e.

one dollar

f.

five cents

4. Colour coins worth twenty cents or more.

5. What is the total value of these coins?

a.    [ ] cents

b.   [ ] cents

c.   [ ] cent

New Syllabus Mentals and Extension 1, Stage On

Naming and Adding Coins
OPTIONAL EXTENSION

1. Name these coins.

a. _____

b. _____

c. _____

2. Colour the coins needed to make these values.

a.  35 cents

b.  $2.55

c.  85 cents

3. Draw two coins for these values.

a.

b.

Coin Values and Totals
OPTIONAL EXTENSION

4. Colour the coins to the value of $3, in each group.

a.

b.

5. Write single coins that have the same value as these.

a.  = $:

b.  = $:

c. + + = $:

d. + = $:

e. + + = $:

6. Colour the coins needed to buy the cake.

$2.35

Shopping with Coins
OPTIONAL EXTENSION

1. What group of coins will buy each item?

a.
$3.60

b.
$1.75

c.
85c

d.
40c

2. Write the value of the coins in each row.

a.  = ☐ cents

b.    = $ ☐

c.   = $ ☐

More Shopping with Coins
OPTIONAL EXTENSION

3. What group of coins will buy each item?

a. 　　**b.**

  85 cents
$1.50　　　$2.55　　$3.60

c. 　　**d.**

4. Add the coins and write their total value

a.   = $ _____

b.  = $ _____

c.    = $ _____

5. Match each coin to its name.

a. 　　**b.**

twenty cents

one dollar

c.

two dollars

fifty cents

d.

e.

five cents

New Syllabus Mentals and Extension 1, Stage On

More About Groups

1. Write the value of these coins in words.

a. _____

b. _____

c. _____

2. Write the order of these coins from smallest to largest in value - 1st to 6th.

3. Add these coins and write a total value.

a.  $\circ$ $:

b.  $\circ$ $:

c.  $\circ$ $:

4. What coins do I need for?

a.  $2.30

b. $4.10

c. $3.25

Use Coins to Buy Goods

5. Colour the coins needed to buy these items.

a.  $2.10

b.  90c

c.  $2.60

6. Round these prices off to the nearest cent.

a. 73 cents _____ b. 24 cents _____

c. 89 cents _____ d. 31 cents _____

e. 52 cents _____ f. 99 cents _____

7. Colour the correct card for these.

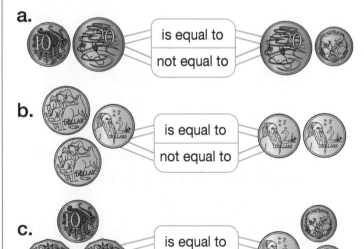

a. is equal to / not equal to

b. is equal to / not equal to

c. is equal to / not equal to

Money – Australian Notes
OPTIONAL EXTENSION

1. Draw a line from each Australian bank note to its name.

a.

b.

c.

d.

e.

- five dollars
- ten dollars
- twenty dollars
- fifty dollars
- one hundred dollars

2. Write the notes in order of value - largest to smallest.

$ _____ $ _____ $ _____ $ _____ $ _____

3. Tick the notes that add to $85.

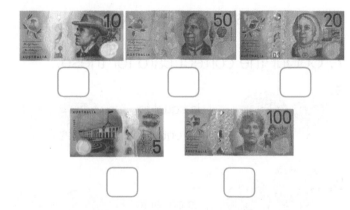

☐ ☐ ☐

☐ ☐

4. Colour the number of coins needed to equal the value of this note.

Working with Australian Notes
OPTIONAL EXTENSION

5. How many $5 notes are needed to equal these notes.

a.    **b.**

☐

c.   ☐

6. Add these notes and write the total.

a.  = $ ☐

b.  = $ ☐

c.  = $ ☐

7. What notes am I?

A black swan can be seen in my watermark. Edith Cowan and David Unaipon are shown on me. I am yellow in colour.

I am a ☐ note.

8. Write the value of these notes and coins.

a.  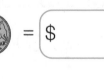 = $ ☐

b.     = $ ☐

New Syllabus Mentals and Extension 1, Stage O

Australian Notes and Coins
OPTIONAL EXTENSION

1. Write the name of these notes in words.

a.  _____

b.  _____

c.  _____

2. Write the value of notes and coins in each group.

a.  = $ _____

b.  = $ _____

c.  = $ _____

3. Order the coins and notes from lowest to highest in value.

4. Write the colour for these notes.

a. $5 _____ **b.** $20 _____

c. $10 _____

Notes and Coins Together
OPTIONAL EXTENSION

5. How much in each group?

a.  = $ _____ :

b.  = $ _____ :

c.  = $ _____ :

6. Colour the notes then write how much they add to in total.

a.  = $ _____

b.  = $ _____

7. How many ten dollar notes are needed to equal each larger note in value.

8. Add the total value of stamps.

 = $ _____

Shopping with Notes and Coins

1. Draw a line to match what some notes can buy.

2. Write these totals as dollars and cents.

a. Ten dollars thirty cents

$:

b. Eighty dollars sixty-five cents

$:

3. Colour the notes and coins needed to buy these items.

a.

b.

4. How many $3 cakes can I buy for thirty dollars?

More Shopping and Comparisons

5. Colour the notes and coins needed to buy these items.

a.

b.

6. Colour the money path for each problem

a.

b.

c.

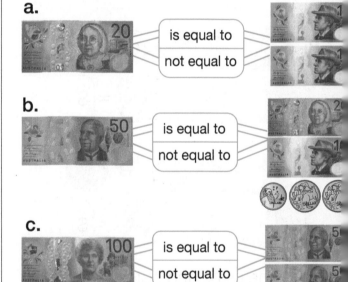

is equal to / not equal to

7. Add the costs of these items and write the totals.

a.

TOTALS $

b.

TOTALS $

8. How many $20 notes in one hundred dollars?

New Syllabus Mentals and Extension 1, Stage On

Know Your Money

1. Colour the notes needed to equal the value of the larger note.

a.

b.

2. What is the value of these coins

a.   cents

b.  cents

3. Write the value of these notes when added together.

TOTAL $ ☐

4. How much do I have?

TOTAL
$ ☐

5. Write the total for the group of notes and coins.

TOTAL
$ ☐

Notes, Coins and Tap 'n' Go

6. Add the notes and coins in each group.

a.  = $ ☐

b.  = $ ☐

7. Write the amount for each fraction.

a. $\frac{1}{2}$ of $10 = ☐ **b.** $\frac{1}{2}$ of $50 = ☐

c. $\frac{1}{4}$ of $20 = ☐ **d.** $\frac{1}{4}$ of $60 = ☐

8. Colour the Tap 'n' Go card.

9. Tick what can be bought using a Tap 'n' Go card.

☐   ☐   ☐   ☐

10. If you are 7 years old, can you have a Tap 'n' Go card?

Yes ☐ or No ☐

11. How many $5 notes are equal to thirty-five dollars. ☐

Extension – Australian Coins and Notes

1. Which coin has 5 kangaroos on the reverse side?

_____

2. Write this coin in words.

_____

_____

3. How many 10 cent coins in $2?

4. What is Australia's largest value coin?

_____

5. Colour the two dollar coin.

6. What coin am I?

> I am a silver coin with a platypus swimming down me. I am?

7. How many ten cent coins in four dollars?

8. Name Australia's largest note.

_____

9. Add these coins.

= $

10. Name this note in words.

_____

_____

11. Colour the coins needed to buy the ice cream.

$3.50

12. Add these notes and coins.

$

13. Write the order of Australian notes, smallest to largest.

14. Write the order of Australian coins, smallest to largest in value.

15. Can I buy a cupcake using a Tap 'n' Go card?

Yes

No

16. Which note is red in colour?

_____

17. How many five dollar notes are equal to one hundred dollars.

New Syllabus Mentals and Extension 1, Stage On

Introducing Length

1. Colour the **longer** one in each group.

a.
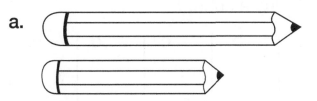

b.

2. Colour the **shorter** one.

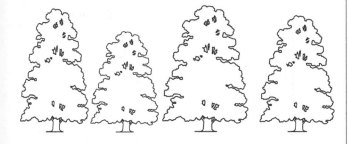

3. Draw a **longer** line and one **shorter** line.

4. Use this square ☐ to find how many are needed to fit along each of these.

a.

b.

c.

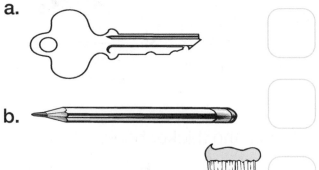

Length

5. Colour the **tallest** tree.

6. Colour the **biggest** tomato.

7. Colour the girl with the **shortest** dress.

8. Order 1-5, the length of these objects from **shortest** to **longest**.

Introducing Length

1. Write the number of paper clips
used to measure these.

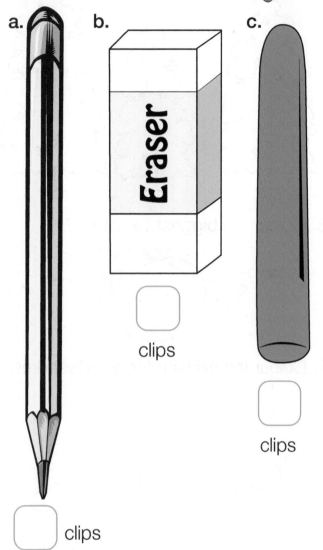

a.   b.   c.

Eraser

clips

clips

clips

2. Use this book to measure these
objects. How many for each one?

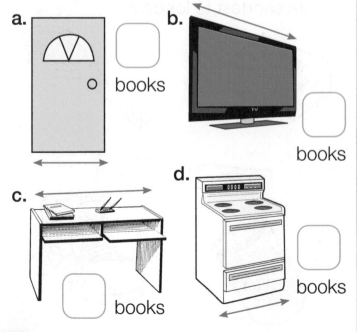

a.   books

b.   books

c.   books

d.   books

Length

3. Measure the length of each line
using a cube.

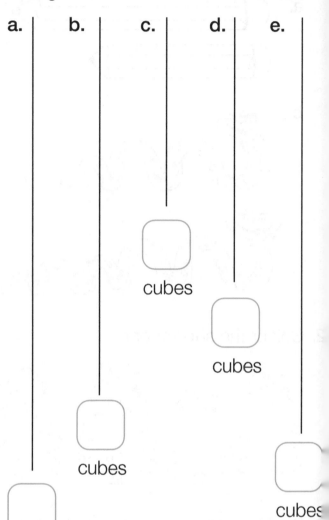

a.   b.   c.   d.   e.

cubes

cubes

cubes

cubes

cubes

4. Use five cent pieces side by side to
measure the length of these objects.

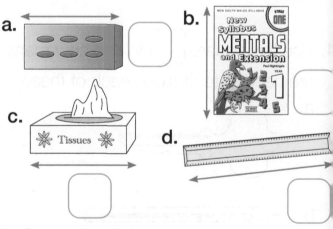

a.

b.

c. Tissues

d.

5. Colour the **thicker** book.

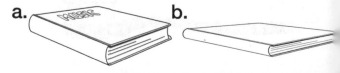

a.   b.

Informal Units of Measuring Length

1. Use mum's tape measure to measure these items at home. Colour the nearest measurement.

a.

longer than a tape measure

shorter than a tape measure

b.

longer than a tape measure

shorter than a tape measure

c.

longer than a tape measure

shorter than a tape measure

d.

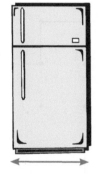

longer than a tape measure

shorter than a tape measure

2. How many tape measures needed across the kitchen?

3. How many tape measures needed across the TV. room?

4. Find something in the house the same length as the tape measure.

_____

5. Name two things shorter than the tape.

_____ _____

Introducing the Metre
OPTIONAL EXTENSION

6. A metre is a formal unit of measuring length. Here is what a metre rule looks like.

Find a metre rule or measure our a metre length to estimate lengths. Colour the nearest measurement.

a.

less than a metre

about one metre

longer than a metre

b.

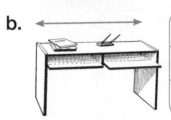

less than a metre

about one metre

longer than a metre

c.

less than a metre

about one metre

longer than a metre

7. Measure out a metre on the floor then find out how many of these fit onto a metre. You might write 1/2 or 1/4 too.

a.

b.

c.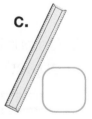

d.

e.

8. Tick the objects that measure more than a metre.

Extension – Length

1. Tick the **shortest** log.

a.    b.

c.   d.

2. Colour the **longest** ribbon.

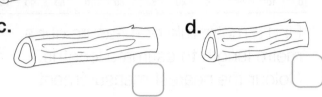

3. How many 5 cent coins will fit on a ruler?

4. Colour the boys with **short** pants.

5. Colour the correct name card for this object's length.

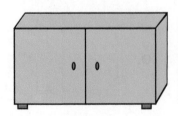

| less than a metre |
| about one metre |
| longer than a metre |

6. Is a skipping rope longer than a car? Tick.

Yes ☐   No ☐

7. About how long is a car? Tick.

4 metres ☐

2 metres ☐

Introducing Area

1. Colour the triangles that are about the same size.

2. Colour the square with the **largest** area

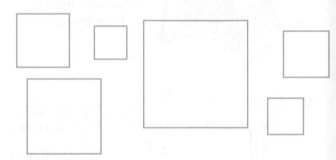

3. Count the squares and colour the **biggest** area.

a.

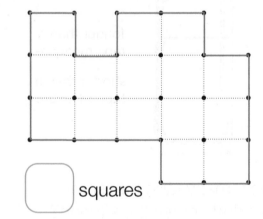

☐ squares

b.

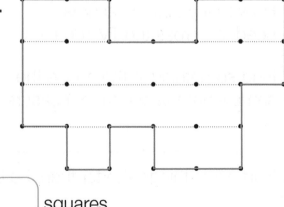

☐ squares

New Syllabus Mentals and Extension 1, Stage On

Comparing Area

1. Colour the shapes with a curved face.

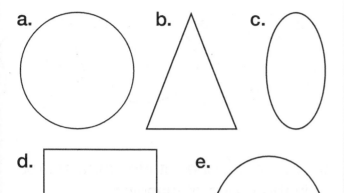

a.   b.   c.

d.   e.

2. Count the tiles in the floor pattern.

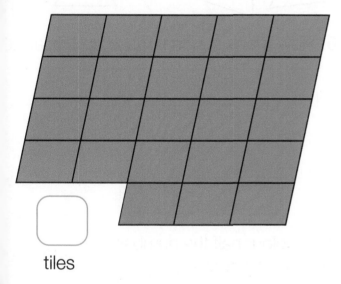

tiles

3. Colour the shape of the tile in the pattern.

4. Colour the shapes smaller than the one in the box.

Comparing Area

5. Count the number of squares in each shape to find the area.

a.

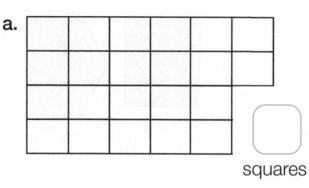

squares

b.

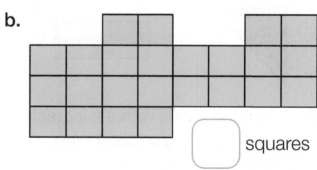

squares

6. Colour the shapes in each group that are **smaller** in area than the one in the box.

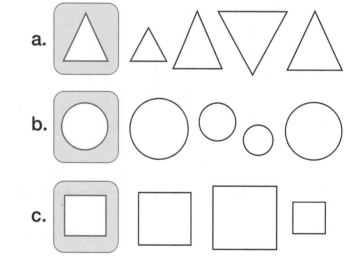

a.

b.

c.

7. Draw a line to connect the ends to make a **closed** area.

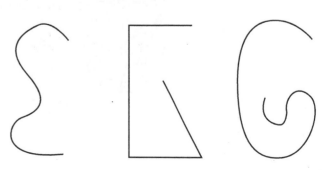

Comparing Area

1. Order the size of area in these shapes from smallest to largest 1 to 5.

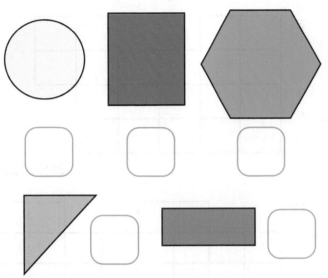

2. Colour the shape with the largest area red and the smallest blue. Count the squares.

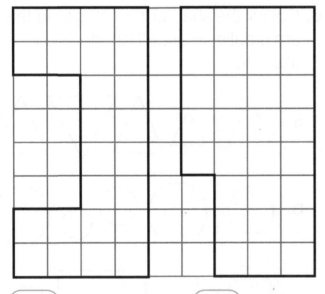

☐ squares ☐ squares

3. Order these in area smallest to largest 1 to 4.

Extension Area

4. Tick the one that has area.

a.   b.   c.

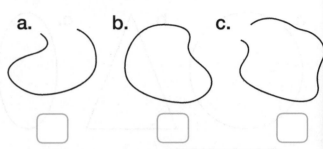

☐   ☐   ☐

5. Colour the one with the **largest** area in this group of triangles.

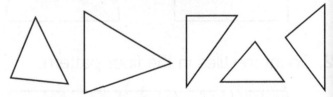

6. How many squares make up this area?

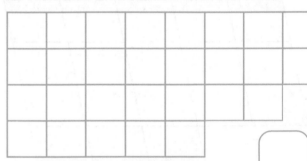

☐ squares

7.a. Colour half the number of area above.

b. How many squares did you colour? ☐

8. Order the areas of the envelopes **smallest** to **largest**.

a.   b.   c.

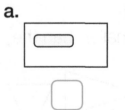

☐   ☐   ☐

9. Which has the **smallest** area in your home. Tick.

Bedroom   Toilet   Kitchen   Lounge Room

Volume

1. Count the blocks in each solid.
Colour the one with the **largest** volume.

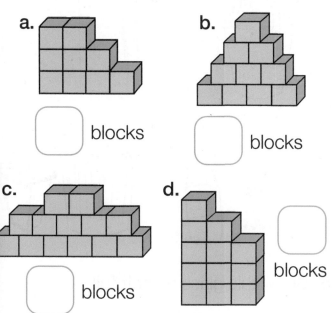

a. ▢ blocks

b. ▢ blocks

c. ▢ blocks

d. ▢ blocks

2. Colour the objects that have volume.

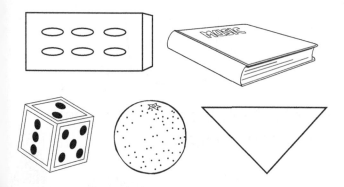

3. Colour the blocks that have the same volume.

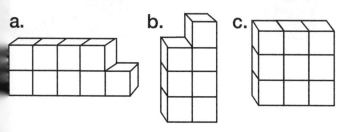

a.

b.

c.

4. Here is a group of blocks.

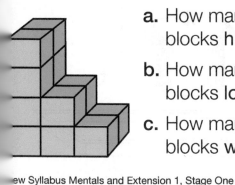
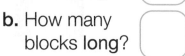

a. How many blocks **high**? ▢

b. How many blocks **long**? ▢

c. How many blocks **wide**? ▢

Volume and Capacity

5. Colour the objects that will hold more than the one in the box.

a.

b.

6. Count how many blocks.

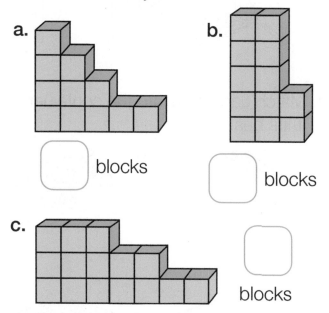

a. ▢ blocks

b. ▢ blocks

c. ▢ blocks

7. Count how many blocks altogether in question 6.  ▢ blocks

Comparing Volume and Capacity

1. Order 1-6, from those holding most to those holding less.

2. Colour the containers that will **NOT** hold water.

3. Match each item into the container it fits best.

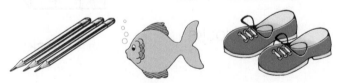

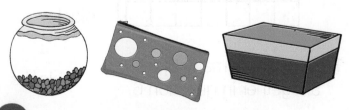

Capacity

4. Colour the object that will hold the **mos**

a.

b.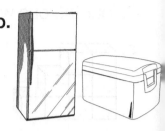

c.

d.

5. Show this glass as **half full**.

6. Order 1 - 4, the containers from **smallest** to **largest**.

7. Colour the objects that will hold water.

  New Syllabus Mentals and Extension 1, Stage On

Volume and Capacity

1. Colour the object that holds less.

a.

b.

c.

d.

e.

f.

2. Order 1-5, smallest to largest, the object's capacity.

3. Count the blocks.

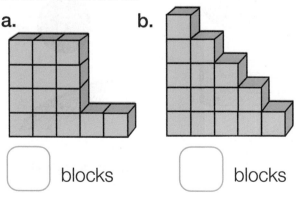

a.

b.

☐ blocks   ☐ blocks

Measuring Capacity

4. How many one litre jugs full are needed to fill a nine litre bucket? Colour the jugs as you count.

5. Colour the glass that will hold the **most** water.

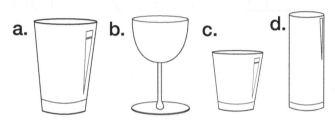

a.   b.   c.   d.

6. Which containers will hold **more** than the first? Tick them.

a.   b.   c.

d.   e.   f.

7. Which containers will hold things other than water? Colour them.

a.   b.   c.

d.   e.

Extension - Volume and Capacity

1. Colour the ball with the **smallest** volume.

2. Tick the blocks with the **largest** volume.

a. 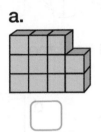 **b.** 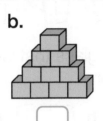 **c.**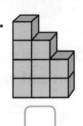

☐ ☐ ☐

3. Tick the **half** full glass.

a.   **b.**   **c.**   **d.**

☐ ☐ ☐ ☐

4. How many full glasses are needed to empty a 2 litre milk bottle? Colour a glass each time you pour.

Total number of full glasses. ☐

5. How many blocks in this solid?

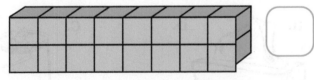 ☐

6. Colour the objects that have volume.

 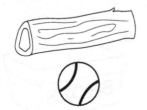

How Heavy?

7. Colour the **heaviest** in each group.

a.  **b.**

c.  **d.**

8. Match the words to the objects.

 heavy

light

 heaviest

9. Order these objects from **lightest** to **heaviest**.

    New Syllabus Mentals and Extension 1, Stage On

Comparing and Measuring Mass

1. Colour the object with the **greatest** mass.

a.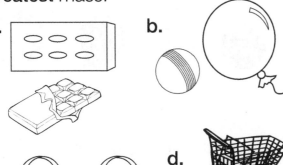

b.

c.
sand   water

d.

2. Colour the **heaviest** object.

3. Is the balance true or false?

a.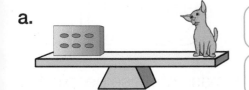

 true

 false

b.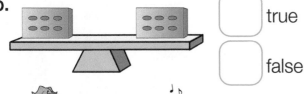

true

false

c.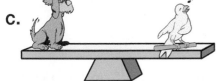

 true

 false

d.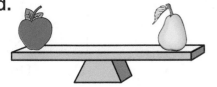

 true

false

Comparing Reactions with Mass

4. Which object is the **heaviest**?

a.

b.

c.

5. Colour the correct arrow to show what happens when the cat on the right gets off the beam.

a.

b.

6. Look at the equal arm balance beam.

The book is _____ than the pencil.

7. Is a cat **heavier** than a canary?

Tick Yes [ ] or No [ ].

Measuring Mass

1. Draw a line from each object to where it should be on the balance scales.

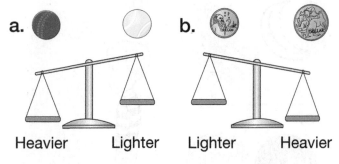

a. **b.**

Heavier   Lighter   Lighter   Heavier

2. Is the balance on the scales true or false? Colour your choice.

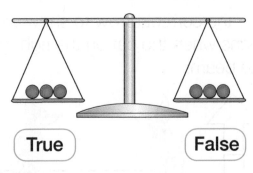

(**True**)   (**False**)

3. Colour the marbles needed to balance the beam.

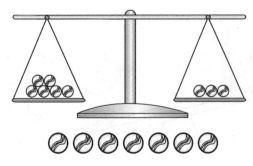

4. Colour the action card for each right tray when objects are added or taken away.

a. **b.**

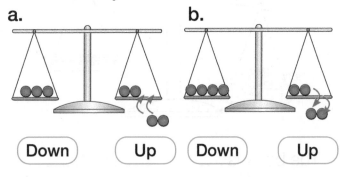

(**Down**) (**Up**) (**Down**) (**Up**)

5. Which is **heavier**, a shoe or a thong?

© Paul Nightingale - Five Senses Education Pty. Ltd.

Extension - Mass

1. Order the fruit **lightest** to **heaviest**.

☐   ☐   ☐   ☐

2. Colour the **heaviest** animal.

3. Is the beam balance true or false?

True ☐

False ☐

4. Colour the one with the **greater** mass in each group.

a.   **b.**   **c.**

5. Order the mass of these people 1-4, lightest to heaviest.

☐   ☐   ☐   ☐

6. If a marble is taken off on the right colour, the arrow tray would move.

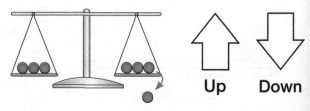

Up   **Down**

New Syllabus Mentals and Extension 1, Stage On

Days of the Week

1. Write the days of the week in order.

_____

Monday

Tuesday

Friday

Sunday

Wednesday

_____

Thursday

I like school days.

_____

Saturday

2. Answer yes or no. Tick ✓

a. Monday comes after Sunday

Yes ◯   No ◯

b. Friday is before Saturday

Yes ◯   No ◯

c. There are 7 days in a week.

Yes ◯   No ◯

3. Tick the weekend pictures.

 ☐    ☐

 ☐    ☐    ☐

4. Write the first day of a school week. _____

5. Write the middle day of the week. _____

Months of the Year

6. Order the months of the year from 1st to 12th.

May ☐   July ☐   April ☐

August ☐   December ☐

January ☐   June ☐   March ☐

November ☐   October ☐

September ☐   February ☐

7. Circle the winter picture.

a.   **b.**

c.   **d.**

8. Write the months of autumn.

_____ _____

_____

9. What is the fifth month of the year? _____

10. How many days in May? ☐

11. Write the last month of the year.

_____

Months of the Year

1. Say the months of the year.

January	February	March
April	May	June
July	August	September
October	November	December

2. Colour the month it is now.

3. Which is the 6th month of the year? _____

4. How many days in June? ☐

5. How many days in July? ☐

6. In which month is your birthday?

_____

7. Write the months of spring.

_____   _____

_____

8. Write the third month of the year.

_____

9. How many months in a year? ☐

10. Write the day and month that it is today.

_____   _____

Day   Month

Know the Months of the Year

11. Write the months of the year in order and the days in each month.

	DAYS
1st _____	
2nd _____	
3rd _____	
4th _____	
5th _____	
6th _____	
7th _____	
8th _____	
9th _____	
10th _____	
11th _____	
12th _____	

12. What is the date for the last day of June? _____

13. Write the date for the first day of May? _____

14. List the months under these headings

a. WINTER   **b.** SUMMER

_____   _____

_____   _____

_____   _____

15. How many days in a leap year? ☐

New Syllabus Mentals and Extension 1, Stage On

Duration of Time

1. Colour the activities that takes about a minute or two to do.

a.

b.

c.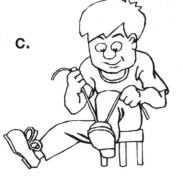

d.

2. How many of these activities can you do in one minute?

a. Clap your hands. ☐   **b.** Skip a rope. ☐

c. Bounce a ball ☐   **d.** Write your name ☐

3. Colour the activity that would take **more** than a day to do.

4. How many days in each season?

a. Summer ☐   **b.** Winter ☐

c. Spring ☐   **d.** Autumn ☐

Extension – Days, Weeks, Months, Time

5. How many days in one week? ☐

6. Fill in the missing days in this week

Sunday, Monday, _____

Wednesday, Thursday, _____

7. Answer Yes or No. Tick

  a. Friday is the last day of a school week. Yes ☐ No ☐

  b. There are 14 days in one fortnight. Yes ☐ No ☐

8. Write the weekend days.

_____ _____

9. How many months in one year? ☐

10. How many days in June? ☐

11. Write the season for these months.

March, April, May _____

12. Write the months for spring.

_____ _____

_____

13. Write the eleventh month of the year.

_____

14. Colour the time card for how long it would take to clean your teeth.

five hours	five minutes

five days

O'Clock Time

1. What time is it?

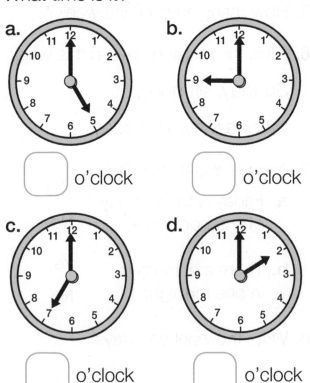

a. ☐ o'clock   b. ☐ o'clock

c. ☐ o'clock   d. ☐ o'clock

2. Show each time on the clock face.

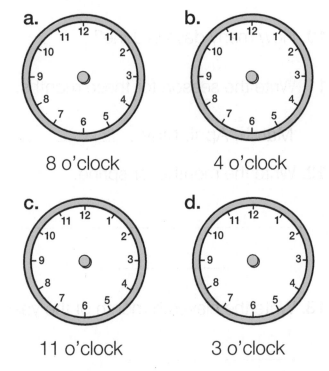

a. 8 o'clock   b. 4 o'clock

c. 11 o'clock   d. 3 o'clock

3. Show the digital time on the clock face.

Half Past the Hour

4. Draw hands on each clock face to show the time.

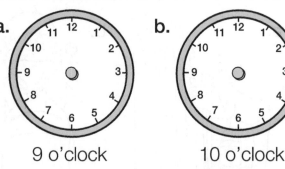

a. 9 o'clock   b. 10 o'clock

c. 2 o'clock   d. 5 o'clock

5. Match the clocks to the times.

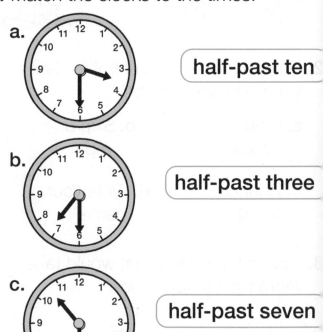

a.

half-past ten

b.

half-past three

c.

half-past seven

6. Show each time on the clock face.

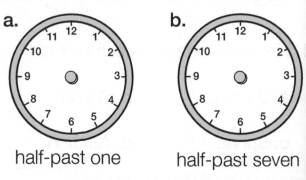

a. half-past one   b. half-past seven

Half Past the Hour

1. What's the digital time?

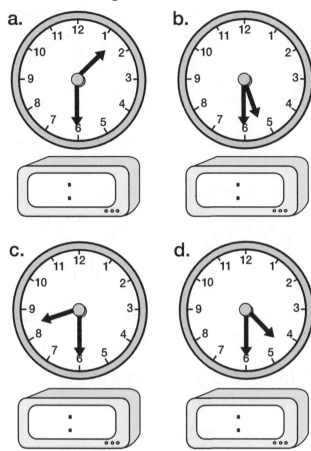

2. Show these digital times on the clock faces.

3. Write these as digital times.

a. half-past six

b. half-past nine

c. half-past four

d. half-past seven

e. half-past eleven

f. half-past eight

Clock face and Digital Time

4. What time is it?

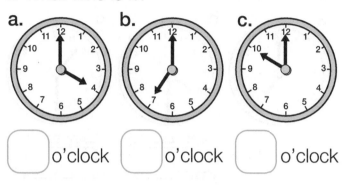

☐ o'clock   ☐ o'clock   ☐ o'clock

 This clock shows half past 2. It can be shown as 2:30

5. Write the digital time showing on each clock face.

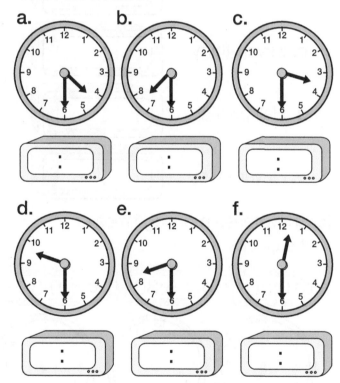

6. Draw hands on the clock face to show each time.

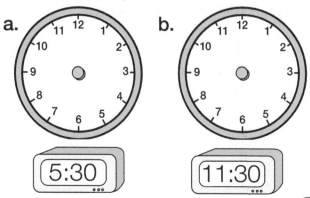

a. 5:30   b. 11:30

Analogue and Digital Time

1. What time is it?

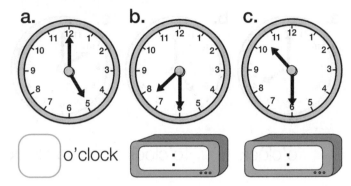

a.

⬜ o'clock

b.

c.

2. Write these morning times on the digital clocks.

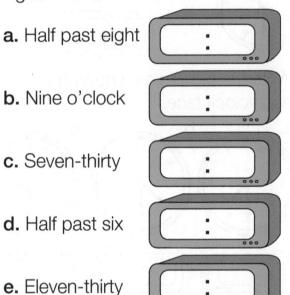

a. Half past eight

b. Nine o'clock

c. Seven-thirty

d. Half past six

e. Eleven-thirty

3. Show these morning times on the clocks.

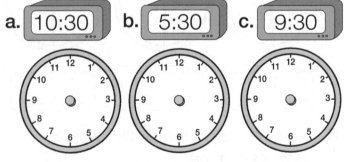

a. `10:30`   b. `5:30`   c. `9:30`

4. Write these times in words

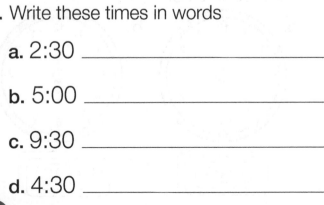

a. 2:30 _____

b. 5:00 _____

c. 9:30 _____

d. 4:30 _____

Half Past Clock Time

5. What time is it?

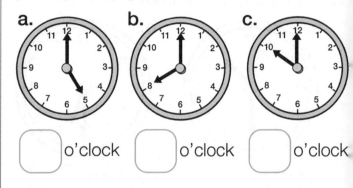

a.

⬜ o'clock

b.

⬜ o'clock

c.

⬜ o'clock

6. Show these times on the clock face.

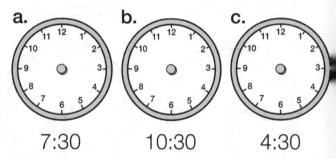

a.   b.   c.

7:30   10:30   4:30

7. Match the digital times to the written times.

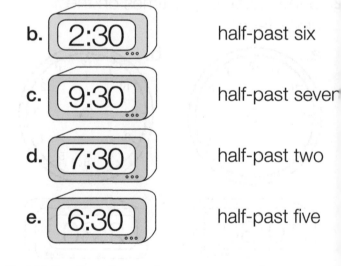

a. `5:30`   half-past nine

b. `2:30`   half-past six

c. `9:30`   half-past seven

d. `7:30`   half-past two

e. `6:30`   half-past five

8. Write the time shown on each clock face.

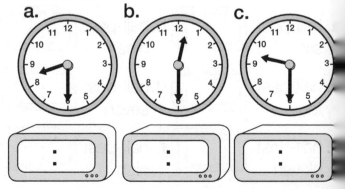

a.   b.   c.

New Syllabus Mentals and Extension 1, Stage On

Analogue and Digital Time

1. Show each time on the clock face.

a. 7:30　　**b.** 10:30　　**c.** 4:30

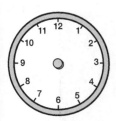  

2. Match the written time to its digital time.

a. half-past seven

b. half-past four

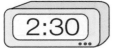

c. half-past ten

d. half-past two

e. half-past eight

3. Write the time on each clock face in digital time.

a. 　　**b.** 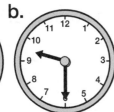　　**c.**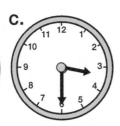

_____ _____ _____

d. 　　**e.** 　　**f.**

_____ _____ _____

Extension – Time

4. Write the time shown on each clock.

a. **b.** **c.**

　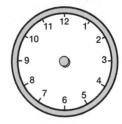

⬜ o'clock ⬜ o'clock ⬜ o'clock

5. Add hands to the clock to show these times.

a. 9 o'clock　　　**b.** 4 o'clock

6. Write the time shown on each clock in words.

a.  _____

b. _____

7. Show these times on the digital clocks.

a. half-past seven

b. half-past eleven

8. Show the clock face time for these.

a. 8:30 　　**b.** 1:30

9. Write these times in words.

a. 12:30 _____

b. 6:00 _____

Two Dimensional Shapes

1. Trace over each shape and draw a line to its name.

circle

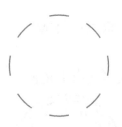

rectangle

square

triangle

2. Colour all the triangles yellow.

Names and Features of 2D Shapes

3. Name the shapes and the number of sides and vertices on each one.

a.
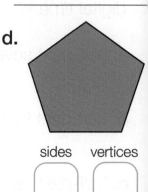
sides ☐
vertices ☐

_____

b.
sides ☐
vertices ☐

_____

c.
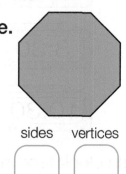
sides ☐
vertices ☐

_____

d.
sides ☐   vertices ☐

_____

e.
sides ☐   vertices ☐

_____

4. Join the dots to draw 2D shapes.

a.

b.

5. Complete this rectangle.

New Syllabus Mentals and Extension 1, Stage On

More 2D Shapes

1. Match the 2D shapes to their names.

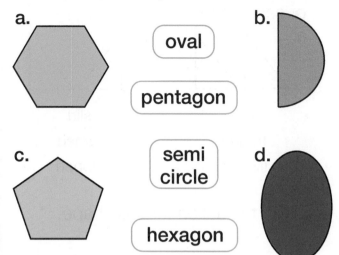

a.

b.

oval

pentagon

semi circle

c.

d.

hexagon

2. Count the vertices and sides on these quadrilaterals.

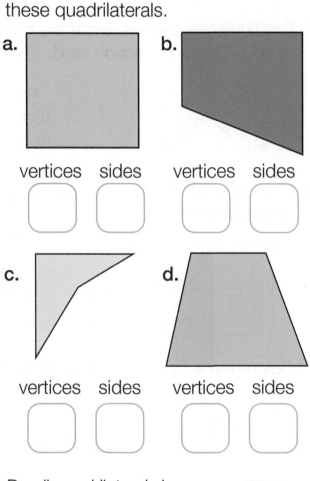

a.

b.

vertices   sides   vertices   sides

c.

d.

vertices   sides   vertices   sides

3. Do all quadrilaterals have 4 sides and 4 vertices?

Yes ☐   No ☐

4. Would all triangles have 3 sides and 3 vertices?

Yes ☐   No ☐

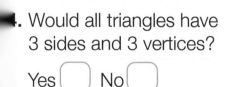

Knowing 2D Shapes and Features

5. Colour all the triangles yellow.

6. How many triangles? ☐

7. Match each shape to its name.

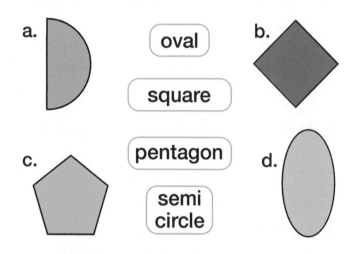

a.

oval

b.

square

pentagon

c.

d.

semi circle

8. Record number of edges and vertices for each shape.

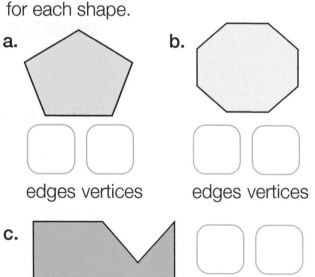

a.

b.

edges vertices

edges vertices

c.

edges vertices

More 2D Shapes

1. Colour the shapes that are the same. Count them and name them.

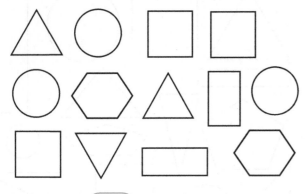

a. There are ⬜ △. Its name is

_____

b. There are ⬜ ⬡. Its name is

_____

c. There are ⬜ ▭. Its name is

_____

2. Trace over the shapes. Match each shape to its name. Colour them.

a.

pentagon

b.

semi-circle

c.

circle

d.

square

Flip, Slide, Turn and Tessellation

3. Colour the card that shows the action of each shape.

a. 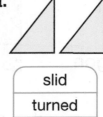 **b.**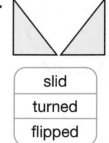

a.	b.
slid	slid
turned	turned
flipped	flipped

4. Label the action for this shape.

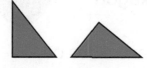 _____

5. Continue this pattern. Draw the next shape. Colour the action card.

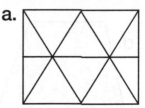

slid
turned
flipped

6. Colour the tile pattern that is NOT a tessellation pattern.

a.  **b.**

7. Colour the shapes that will tessellate.

8. Draw the tile for this tessellation.

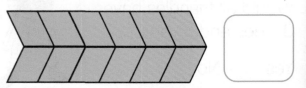

Extension 2D Shapes and Actions

1. Name this 2D shape.

_____

2. How many sides on a hexagon? sides

3. How many vertices on an octagon?  vertices

4. Is this a triangle? Yes or No. Tick.

Yes ☐   No ☐

5. Colour the pentagon.

6. Colour the quadrilaterals.

 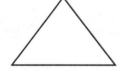

 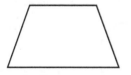

7. How many sides on a quadrilateral?

8. Are all 4 sided 2D shapes quadrilaterals?   Yes ☐   No ☐

9. Colour the tiles that could make a tessellation pattern.

3 Dimensional Objects

10. Match the objects to their names.

a.

rectangular prism

b.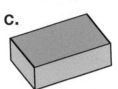

sphere

c.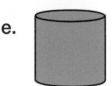

square pyramid

d.

cylinder

e.

cube

11. Colour the everyday objects that are **cylinders**.

3D Objects, Names and Features

1. Name these 3D objects.

a.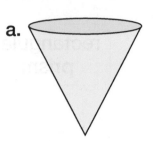

b.

_____   _____

c.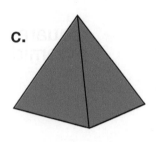

d.

_____

2. Colour the objects that will **roll**.

3D Objects and Features

3. Match 3D objects to their names.

a.
b.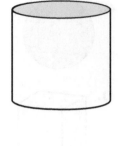

cone

cube

cylinder

sphere

square pyramid

rectangular prism

c.
d.

e.

f.

4. Colour the cylinders.

5. Colour the 3D objects that will stack easily.

New Syllabus Mentals and Extension 1, Stage On

3D Faces, Edges and Vertices

1. Count the faces, edges, corners and curved surfaces.

a.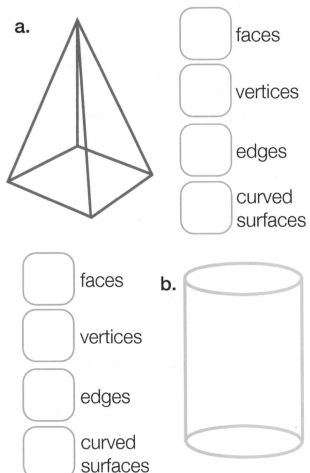

⬜ faces

⬜ vertices

⬜ edges

⬜ curved surfaces

⬜ faces

b.

⬜ vertices

⬜ edges

⬜ curved surfaces

2. Count the number of faces on each 3D object.

a. 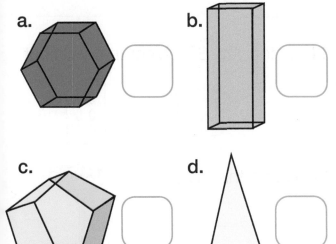 ⬜

b. ⬜

c. ⬜

d. ⬜

3. Name this 3D object.

 _____

3D Objects, Faces and Features

4. Match each 3D object to one of its faces.

a.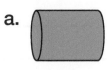

b.

c.

d.

e.

5. Match the 3D objects to their names.

a.

⬭ sphere

b.

⬭ cylinder

c.

⬭ cube

d.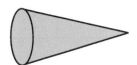

⬭ rectangular prism

6. Name this 3D object.

_____

3D Objects/2D Shapes

1. Match the top, side and front views to a 3D shape.

a.

b.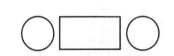

c.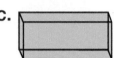

d.

2. Colour the objects that will **float**.

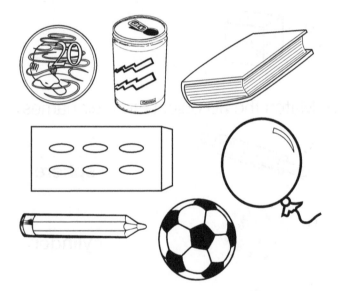

3. Draw an object that will **sink**.

4. Name this 3D object.

 _____

Extension 3D Objects

5. Name this object.

 _____

6. Colour the cylinder.

7. Colour the rectangular prism.

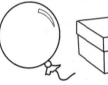  

8. How many faces on a cube?

9. Does a cone have a curved surface?

Tick Yes ☐ or No ☐

10. Name this object.

 _____
_____

11. Colour the 3D object that will float.

12. Name this 3D object.

_____

13. Have many faces on a regular pyramid?

14. Is this dice a cube?

Tick Yes or No

New Syllabus Mentals and Extension 1, Stage On

Position

1. Colour the arrows pointing to the **right**.

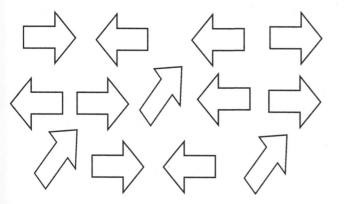

2. Colour the **middle** can of soft drink.

3. Draw an X under the **closest** tree.
Circle the **furthest** one.

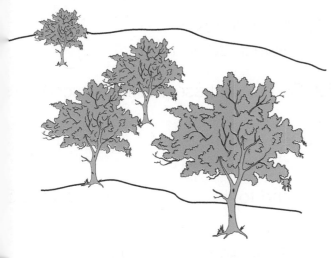

4. Draw a dish in **front** of the cat and a mouse **behind** it.

Position and Direction

5. Follow the directions to plot a path on the grid.

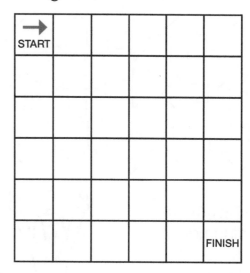

Right 4 squares

Down 3 squares

Left 3 squares

Down 2 squares

Right 4 squares

6. Match a rosette to each runner.

7. Circle the **first** runner.

8. Colour or tick, the **left** one in each pair. (Look closely)

a.

b.

c.

d.

Position and Direction

1. Colour the arrows pointing **up** red, and those pointing **down**, yellow.

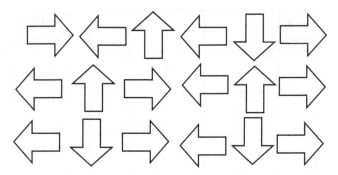

2. How many arrows are pointing right? ⬜

3. How many arrows are pointing left? ⬜

4. How many arrows in total? ⬜

5. Follow the directions and colour the path to reach the beach.

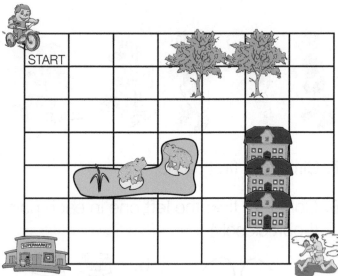

Ahead 2, down 3, left 2, down 2, right 4, up 3, right 2, down 4.

BEACH

6. Colour the **right** foot and **left** shoe.

Position

5	10	15	20	25	30
35	40	45	50	55	60
65	70	75	80	85	90
	95	100			

7. What number is above 35? ⬜

8. What number is below 80? ⬜

9. What number is next to 75 on the left? ⬜

10. What number is next to 50 on the right? ⬜

11. What number is between 20 and 30? ⬜

12. Complete these position descriptions

   a. 45 is to the left of ⬜ and ⬜

   and to the _____ of 40 and 35

   b. 50 is below ⬜ and

   above ⬜ and ⬜.

13. What number is above 95? ⬜

14. Count by 10s, then colour each of those from 10 to 100.

15. How many numbers did you colour? ⬜

New Syllabus Mentals and Extension 1, Stage On

Position and Location Maps

1. Colour a path from Ali's house to the park.

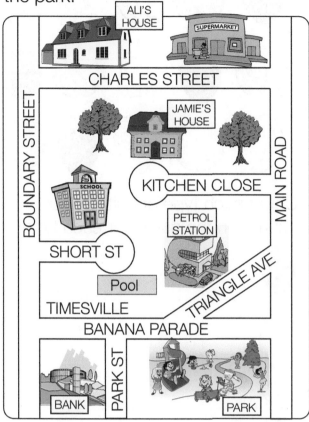

2. Who lives in Kitchen Close?

_____

3. Is the Service Station in Banana Parade? Yes ◯ No ◯

4. What is on the corner of Main Road and Charles Street?

_____

5. Are the school and the pool in Short Street? Yes ◯ No ◯

6. On what street does Ali live?

_____

7. Draw a path from Jamie's house to school.

8. On what street is the park?

_____

9. What can be found on the corner of Boundary Street and Banana Pde?

_____

Extension Position and Maps

10. What colour is the **middle** glass?

 _____

11. Colour the arrow pointing **right**.

12. Colour the **left** foot.

13. Colour what is on the **left** of the elephant.

14.

3	6	9	12	15	18
0	5	10	13	17	19
20	21	27	33	37	42
43	44	46	47	48	50

a. What is above 13? ◯

b. What is below 9? ◯

c. What is to the left of 5? ◯

d. What number is to the right of 17? ◯

e. What number is between 33 and 42? ◯

15. Match the position of the runners to the correct place rosette.

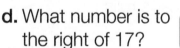

 4th   2nd   5th   middle

Interpreting Data

Collecting Data

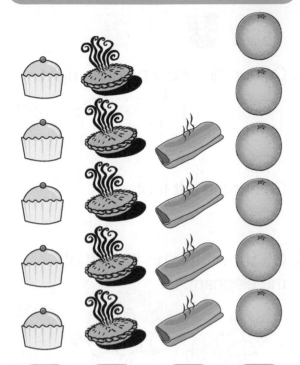

1.

2. What was the most popular item sold at the tuck shop?

3. How many sausage rolls were sold?

4. How many more oranges were sold than cup-cakes?

5. Which items sold the same amount? Colour them.

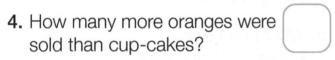

6. Which item would you buy?

_____

7. How many items in total were sold at the Tuck Shop?

8. Count each type of fruit. Colour a square on the graph for each type.

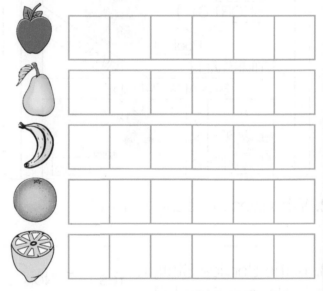

9. Which is the **most** fruit? _____

10. How many bananas?

11. How many apples?

12. Which fruits have the **same** amount?

_____   _____

13. How many **more** oranges than lemons?

14. Which fruit do you like best?

_____

15. How many pieces of fruit altogether?

New Syllabus Mentals and Extension 1, Stage On

Reading Data

Teacher's Drinks

1. What drink do the teachers like **most**?

_____

2. How many teachers drink water? ☐

3. How many teachers drink tea? ☐

4. How many **more** teachers drink tea than juice? ☐

5. Which drinks are **equally** popular?

_____

6. How many **more** teachers drink soft drink than juice? ☐

7. How many teachers are shown on the graph altogether? ☐

8. What does your teacher drink?

_____

Collecting Data and Picture Graph

9. Count each group of animals then colour a square on the graph for each animal.

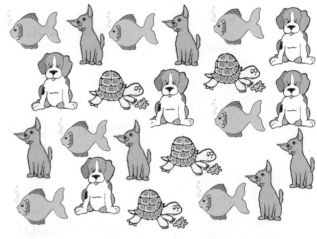

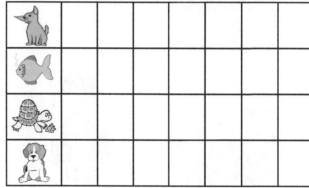

🐱						
🐟						
🐢						
🐶						

10. How many dogs are there? ☐

11. Are there **more** cats than turtles? Yes ☐ No ☐

12. How many **more** cats are there than turtles? ☐

13. Of which animal is there the **most**?

_____

14. Of which animal is there the **least**?

_____

15. How many **more** fish are there than dogs? ☐

16. How many **more** fish are there than turtles? ☐

17. How many animals in total? ☐

18. Add the animal you have or like best to the picture graph.

Chance of Happening

1. Match the chance cards to describe events.

a.

b.

c.

d.

| will happen |
| might happen |
| won't happen |

2. Colour the chance card for these statements.

a. Mum will cook dinner tonight.

| will happen |
| won't happen |
| might happen |

b. I will go to school on Saturday

| will happen |
| won't happen |
| might happen |

c. Dad will win lotto.

| will happen |
| won't happen |
| might happen |

d.

| will happen |
| won't happen |
| might happen |

Chance – Possible, Never, Unlikely

3. Colour the people, animal or monster that will **never** visit your school.

4. Draw a picture of something that will happen tomorrow.

Chance and Results

5. Roll a dice 10 times. Draw the number that comes up on each throw.

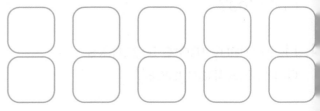

6. Draw the number on the dice that turned up the most.

7. Draw the number that turned up the least.

8. Draw the number on the dice that turned up three or four times.

9. Draw the number that only turned up once.

10. Did any number not turn up at all?

_____

New Syllabus Mentals and Extension 1, Stage On

Answers

p4
1.a. 6 b. 8 c. 4 d. 9 e. 3 f. 10
2.a. 5/7 b. 6/3/2
3.a. 5/7 b. 8/10
4. 9 5.a. 4,5 b. 9,10
6.a. fifteen - matches b. eleven - stars
  c. sixteen - bananas c. fourteen - oranges
7.a. 17 b. 12 c. 19 d. 13 e. 16 f. 20
8.a. 15 b. 12
9.a. 15,17,19 b. 17,16,13
10.a. 11 b. 7 c. 4

p5
1. 10,11,13,14
2.a. 15,16,18,19,20 b. 11,13,14,15
3.a. 17,18 b. 11,12 c. 13,14 d. 6,7
4.a. 7 b. 18 c. 11 d. 14
5. 18 hearts, 12 tennis balls
6.a. seventeen b. eight c. thirteen
7.a. 8 b. 4 c. 1
8.a. 25 b. 30 c. 21 d. 20 e. 27 f. 11
  g. 29 h. 12
9.a. 13 b. 15 c. 16
10.a. 28 b. 27
11.a. 14,16,22 b. 19,17,16
12.a. 3 b. 0 zero

p6
Extension
1.a. zero b. six c. twenty-one
  d. twenty-seven
2.a. 9,10,12 b. 20,21,23
3.a. 23 b. 30 c. 28 d. 19
4.a. 22 b. 19 c. 28 d. 19
5.a. 18 b. 23
6.a. 25,26 b. 29,30
7. twenty-five (25) nineteen (19) eight (8)
  twenty-nine (29) thirty (30) twenty-two (22)
8.a. is not equal to b. is less than
  c. is the same as
9.a. 25,26 b. 10,11 c. 13,14 d. 8,9
10. 16 11. 29 12. twenty-six

p7
1.a. 40 b. 30
2.a. 40 b. 60 c. 90 d. 70 e. 80 f. 30
  g. 20 h. 5
3.a. 50 b. 40
4. +10
5. 20/40//50/60/70/80/100/110
6. 50 7.
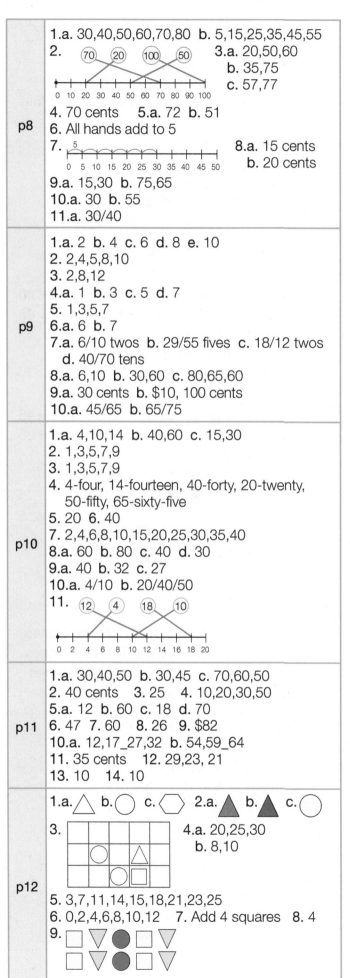
8.a. 0,30,40,60 b. 50,60,90
9.a. 30/50 b. 70/90 c. 40/60 d. 60/80
10. 100
11.a. 57,67 b. 72,82 c. 29,39 d. 18/28
12. is not the same

p8
1.a. 30,40,50,60,70,80 b. 5,15,25,35,45,55
2. (70) (20) (100) (50)
3.a. 20,50,60
  b. 35,75
  c. 57,77
4. 70 cents 5.a. 72 b. 51
6. All hands add to 5
7.
8.a. 15 cents
  b. 20 cents
9.a. 15,30 b. 75,65
10.a. 30 b. 55
11.a. 30/40

p9
1.a. 2 b. 4 c. 6 d. 8 e. 10
2. 2,4,5,8,10
3. 2,8,12
4.a. 1 b. 3 c. 5 d. 7
5. 1,3,5,7
6.a. 6 b. 7
7.a. 6/10 twos b. 29/55 fives c. 18/12 twos
  d. 40/70 tens
8.a. 6,10 b. 30,60 c. 80,65,60
9.a. 30 cents b. $10, 100 cents
10.a. 45/65 b. 65/75

p10
1.a. 4,10,14 b. 40,60 c. 15,30
2. 1,3,5,7,9
3. 1,3,5,7,9
4. 4-four, 14-fourteen, 40-forty, 20-twenty,
  50-fifty, 65-sixty-five
5. 20 6. 40
7. 2,4,6,8,10,15,20,25,30,35,40
8.a. 60 b. 80 c. 40 d. 30
9.a. 40 b. 32 c. 27
10.a. 4/10 b. 20/40/50
11. (12) (4) (18) (10)

p11
1.a. 30,40,50 b. 30,45 c. 70,60,50
2. 40 cents 3. 25 4. 10,20,30,50
5.a. 12 b. 60 c. 18 d. 70
6. 47 7. 60 8. 26 9. $82
10.a. 12,17_27,32 b. 54,59_64
11. 35 cents 12. 29,23, 21
13. 10 14. 10

p12
1.a. △ b. ○ c. ⬡ 2.a. ▲ b. ▲ c. ○
3.
4.a. 20,25,30
  b. 8,10
5. 3,7,11,14,15,18,21,23,25
6. 0,2,4,6,8,10,12 7. Add 4 squares 8. 4
9.

   79

Answers

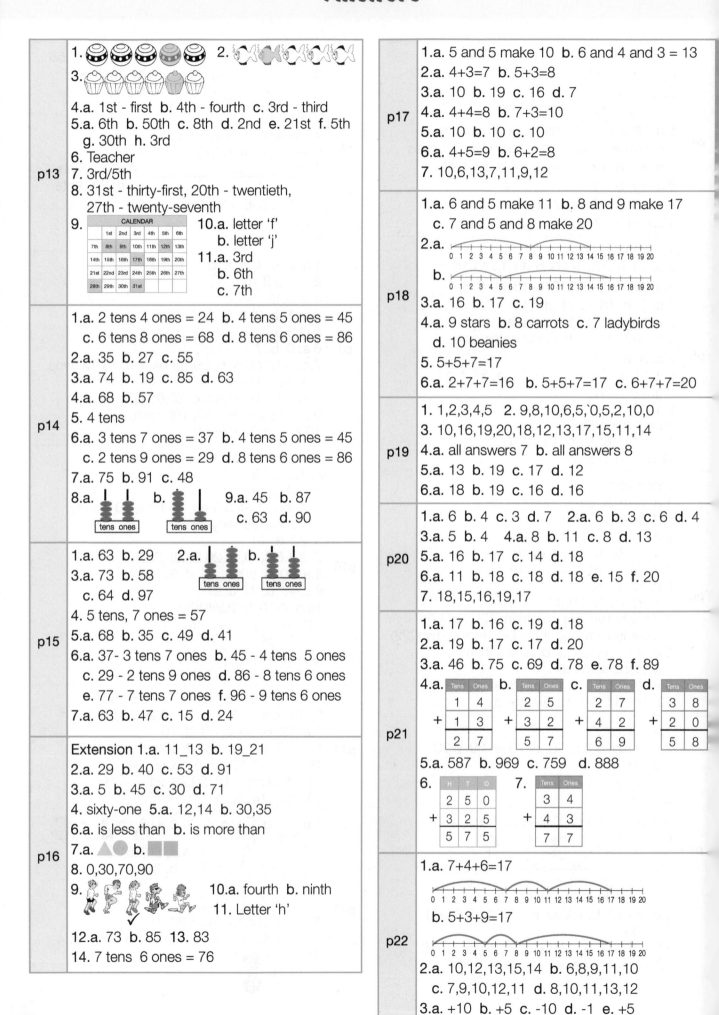

p13

1. 🪩🪩🪩🪩🪩   2. 🐟🐟🐟🐟🐟🐟
3. 🧁🧁🧁🧁🧁
4.a. 1st - first b. 4th - fourth c. 3rd - third
5.a. 6th b. 50th c. 8th d. 2nd e. 21st f. 5th
  g. 30th h. 3rd
6. Teacher
7. 3rd/5th
8. 31st - thirty-first, 20th - twentieth,
  27th - twenty-seventh
9.

CALENDAR					
1st	2nd	3rd	4th	5th	6th
7th	8th	9th	10th	11th	12th	13th
14th	15th	16th	17th	18th	19th	20th
21st	22nd	23rd	24th	25th	26th	27th
28th	29th	30th	31st		

10.a. letter 'f'
  b. letter 'j'
11.a. 3rd
  b. 6th
  c. 7th

p14

1.a. 2 tens 4 ones = 24 b. 4 tens 5 ones = 45
  c. 6 tens 8 ones = 68 d. 8 tens 6 ones = 86
2.a. 35 b. 27 c. 55
3.a. 74 b. 19 c. 85 d. 63
4.a. 68 b. 57
5. 4 tens
6.a. 3 tens 7 ones = 37 b. 4 tens 5 ones = 45
  c. 2 tens 9 ones = 29 d. 8 tens 6 ones = 86
7.a. 75 b. 91 c. 48
8.a.   b.   9.a. 45 b. 87
           c. 63 d. 90
tens ones   tens ones

p15

1.a. 63 b. 29   2.a.   b.
3.a. 73 b. 58
  c. 64 d. 97   tens ones   tens ones
4. 5 tens, 7 ones = 57
5.a. 68 b. 35 c. 49 d. 41
6.a. 37- 3 tens 7 ones b. 45 - 4 tens 5 ones
  c. 29 - 2 tens 9 ones d. 86 - 8 tens 6 ones
  e. 77 - 7 tens 7 ones f. 96 - 9 tens 6 ones
7.a. 63 b. 47 c. 15 d. 24

p16

Extension 1.a. 11_13 b. 19_21
2.a. 29 b. 40 c. 53 d. 91
3.a. 5 b. 45 c. 30 d. 71
4. sixty-one 5.a. 12,14 b. 30,35
6.a. is less than b. is more than
7.a. 🔺⚫ b. ◼◼
8. 0,30,70,90
9. [running figures with checkmark]   10.a. fourth b. ninth
                     11. Letter 'h'
12.a. 73 b. 85 13. 83
14. 7 tens 6 ones = 76

p17

1.a. 5 and 5 make 10 b. 6 and 4 and 3 = 13
2.a. 4+3=7 b. 5+3=8
3.a. 10 b. 19 c. 16 d. 7
4.a. 4+4=8 b. 7+3=10
5.a. 10 b. 10 c. 10
6.a. 4+5=9 b. 6+2=8
7. 10,6,13,7,11,9,12

p18

1.a. 6 and 5 make 11 b. 8 and 9 make 17
  c. 7 and 5 and 8 make 20
2.a. [number line 0-20]
  b. [number line 0-20]
3.a. 16 b. 17 c. 19
4.a. 9 stars b. 8 carrots c. 7 ladybirds
  d. 10 beanies
5. 5+5+7=17
6.a. 2+7+7=16 b. 5+5+7=17 c. 6+7+7=20

p19

1. 1,2,3,4,5 2. 9,8,10,6,5,`0,5,2,10,0
3. 10,16,19,20,18,12,13,17,15,11,14
4.a. all answers 7 b. all answers 8
5.a. 13 b. 19 c. 17 d. 12
6.a. 18 b. 19 c. 16 d. 16

p20

1.a. 6 b. 4 c. 3 d. 7   2.a. 6 b. 3 c. 6 d. 4
3.a. 5 b. 4   4.a. 8 b. 11 c. 8 d. 13
5.a. 16 b. 17 c. 14 d. 18
6.a. 11 b. 18 c. 18 d. 18 e. 15 f. 20
7. 18,15,16,19,17

p21

1.a. 17 b. 16 c. 19 d. 18
2.a. 19 b. 17 c. 17 d. 20
3.a. 46 b. 75 c. 69 d. 78 e. 78 f. 89
4.a.

Tens	Ones
1	4
+ 1	3
2	7

b.

Tens	Ones
2	5
+ 3	2
5	7

c.

Tens	Ones
2	7
+ 4	2
6	9

d.

Tens	Ones
3	8
+ 2	0
5	8

5.a. 587 b. 969 c. 759 d. 888
6.

H	T	O
2	5	0
+ 3	2	5
5	7	5

7.

Tens	Ones
3	4
+ 4	3
7	7

p22

1.a. 7+4+6=17
[number line 0-20]
  b. 5+3+9=17
[number line 0-20]
2.a. 10,12,13,15,14 b. 6,8,9,11,10
  c. 7,9,10,12,11 d. 8,10,11,13,12
3.a. +10 b. +5 c. -10 d. -1 e. +5

New Syllabus Mentals and Extension 1, Stage Or

Answers

p22
Extension 1. 7 2. 14 3. 13 4. 14
5. 2+4+7+6=19 6.a. 7 b. 7
7. 8+7+3=18
8.a. 17,15,19,13,11,14,16,12
  b. 12,9,16,11,7,13,15,8,10,4,10,6
9.a. 47 b. 87 c. 678

p23
1.a. 9-3=6 b. 10-5=5
2.a. cross of 3 leaves 4 b. cross off 2 leaves 7
3.a. 4 b. 6 c. 6 d. 3 e. 6 f. 5
4. 9-3=6 5. 9-6=3 6. 16-13=3
7. 16-11=5 8.a. 7 b. 6 c. 6

p24
1.a. 7-2=5 b. 8-5=3 c. 10-3=7
2. 12-5=7 (cross off 5 flowers)
3.a. 4 b. 6 c. 8 d. 90 cents
4. 8,6,4,2,0,10,10,10,10,10
5.a. 6,5,4,3,2,1,0 b. 9,8,7,6,5,4,3,2,1,0
6. 10-7=3

p25
1.a. 4-2=2 b. 8-3=5 c. 9-3=6
2.a. 14-5=9 b. 13-6=7
3.a. 7-2=5 b. 14-4=10
4.a. 7-2=5 b. 10-6=4 c. 10-2=8
5.a. 13 b. 14 c. 6 d. 12

p26
1.a. 9-6=3 b. 6-5=1 c. 8-5=3
2.a. 10-7=3
  0 1 2 3 4 5 6 7 8 9 10
  b. 9-8=1
  0 1 2 3 4 5 6 7 8 9 10
3.a. 10-7=3 b. 20-17=3
4.a. 13-5=8 b. 15-11=4 c. 20-13=7
  d. 18-16=2
5.a. 12 b. 6 c. 13 d. 6 e. 7 f. 9
6.a. 8,10,11,13,15,16 b. 5,7,8,10,12,13
  c. 6,8,9,11,13,14

p27
1.a. 8 b. 9 c. 10 d. 8 e. 8 f. 10
   -5   -5   -6   -1   -6   -7
   ___   ___   ___   ___   ___   ___
    3   4   4   7   2   3
2.a. 6 b. 3 c. 7 d. 13 e. 12 f. 11
3.a. 14 b. 5
4.a. 12 b. 21 c. 23 d. 33 e. 46 f. 35
5.a. 28-13=15 b. 77-24=53   6.a. 554

Tens	Ones
2	8
- 1	3
1	5

Tens	Ones
7	7
- 2	4
5	3

b. 262

7.
Tens	Ones
7	6
- 2	2
5	4

p28
1.a. 12-6=6   9-8=1   2.a. 6 b. 5 c. 3
3.a. 5 b. 4 c. 2
                        d. 9
4. 4,3,8,5,6 5.a. 25 b. 324
6.a. 12/12 b. 16/16 c. 19/19 d. 22/22
7.a. 6/6 b. 9/9 c. 8/8
8.a. is equal to b. not equal to c. not equal to
  d. is equal to
9.a. 8,14,11,16,21,24 b. 4,10,7,12,17,20
  c. 7,13,10,15,20,23

p29
Extension 1. 7 2. 3 3. 16-5=11
4. 10-7=7 5.a. 5 b. 9 c. 15 d. 11
6.a. 7 b. 12 c. 23 d. 13   7. 16-11=5
8. 7-5=2
  0 1 2 3 4 5 6 7 8 9 10
9.a. 6 b. 7 10.a.

Tens	Ones
2	6
- 1	4
1	2

b.

H	T	O
4	2	5
- 1	1	1
3	1	4

11.a.
	7	
8		5
	4	

b.
	12	
10		2
	4	

12.a. 22,26,3,25,14 b. 31,35,12,34,23

p30
1. 2 groups of 6 make 12
2.a. 3 groups of 5 make 15
  b. 2 groups of 6 make 12
3. 4/4/4/4. 3 rows of 4 make 12
4. 5 groups of 2 make 10
5.a. 4/4. 2 rows of 4 make 8
  b. 3/3/3. 3 rows of 3 make 9
6.a. 2 rows of 3   3 rows of 4

p31
1. 4 groups of 3 = 12
2. 3 groups of 2 = 6 3. Colour 2 mittens
by 6 pairs
                           (12 mittens in total)
4. 6 pairs
5.a. 4 groups of 3 dogs make 12
  b. 3 groups of 5 frogs make 15
6.a. 2 rows of 4 birds make 8
  b. 4 rows of 2 birds make 8

Answers

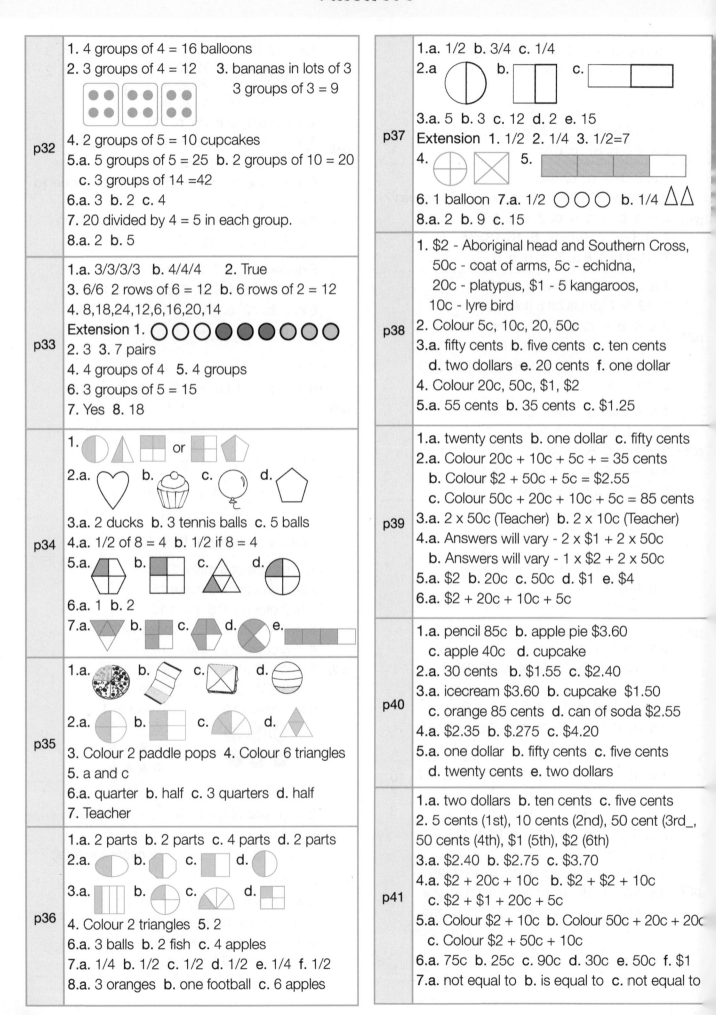

p32
1. 4 groups of 4 = 16 balloons
2. 3 groups of 4 = 12   3. bananas in lots of 3
   3 groups of 3 = 9
4. 2 groups of 5 = 10 cupcakes
5.a. 5 groups of 5 = 25 b. 2 groups of 10 = 20
   c. 3 groups of 14 = 42
6.a. 3 b. 2 c. 4
7. 20 divided by 4 = 5 in each group.
8.a. 2 b. 5

p33
1.a. 3/3/3/3 b. 4/4/4   2. True
3. 6/6 2 rows of 6 = 12 b. 6 rows of 2 = 12
4. 8,18,24,12,6,16,20,14
Extension 1.
2. 3 3. 7 pairs
4. 4 groups of 4 5. 4 groups
6. 3 groups of 5 = 15
7. Yes 8. 18

p34
1.
2.a.   b.   c.   d.
3.a. 2 ducks b. 3 tennis balls c. 5 balls
4.a. 1/2 of 8 = 4 b. 1/2 if 8 = 4
5.a.   b.   c.   d.
6.a. 1 b. 2
7.a.   b.   c.   d.   e.

p35
1.a.   b.   c.   d.
2.a.   b.   c.   d.
3. Colour 2 paddle pops 4. Colour 6 triangles
5. a and c
6.a. quarter b. half c. 3 quarters d. half
7. Teacher

p36
1.a. 2 parts b. 2 parts c. 4 parts d. 2 parts
2.a.   b.   c.   d.
3.a.   b.   c.   d.
4. Colour 2 triangles 5. 2
6.a. 3 balls b. 2 fish c. 4 apples
7.a. 1/4 b. 1/2 c. 1/2 d. 1/2 e. 1/4 f. 1/2
8.a. 3 oranges b. one football c. 6 apples

p37
1.a. 1/2 b. 3/4 c. 1/4
2.a.   b.   c.
3.a. 5 b. 3 c. 12 d. 2 e. 15
Extension 1. 1/2 2. 1/4 3. 1/2=7
4.   5.
6. 1 balloon 7.a. 1/2   b. 1/4
8.a. 2 b. 9 c. 15

p38
1. $2 - Aboriginal head and Southern Cross,
   50c - coat of arms, 5c - echidna,
   20c - platypus, $1 - 5 kangaroos,
   10c - lyre bird
2. Colour 5c, 10c, 20, 50c
3.a. fifty cents b. five cents c. ten cents
   d. two dollars e. 20 cents f. one dollar
4. Colour 20c, 50c, $1, $2
5.a. 55 cents b. 35 cents c. $1.25

p39
1.a. twenty cents b. one dollar c. fifty cents
2.a. Colour 20c + 10c + 5c + = 35 cents
   b. Colour $2 + 50c + 5c = $2.55
   c. Colour 50c + 20c + 10c + 5c = 85 cents
3.a. 2 x 50c (Teacher) b. 2 x 10c (Teacher)
4.a. Answers will vary - 2 x $1 + 2 x 50c
   b. Answers will vary - 1 x $2 + 2 x 50c
5.a. $2 b. 20c c. 50c d. $1 e. $4
6.a. $2 + 20c + 10c + 5c

p40
1.a. pencil 85c b. apple pie $3.60
   c. apple 40c d. cupcake
2.a. 30 cents b. $1.55 c. $2.40
3.a. icecream $3.60 b. cupcake $1.50
   c. orange 85 cents d. can of soda $2.55
4.a. $2.35 b. $.275 c. $4.20
5.a. one dollar b. fifty cents c. five cents
   d. twenty cents e. two dollars

p41
1.a. two dollars b. ten cents c. five cents
2. 5 cents (1st), 10 cents (2nd), 50 cent (3rd_,
   50 cents (4th), $1 (5th), $2 (6th)
3.a. $2.40 b. $2.75 c. $3.70
4.a. $2 + 20c + 10c b. $2 + $2 + 10c
   c. $2 + $1 + 20c + 5c
5.a. Colour $2 + 10c b. Colour 50c + 20c + 20c
   c. Colour $2 + 50c + 10c
6.a. 75c b. 25c c. 90c d. 30c e. 50c f. $1
7.a. not equal to b. is equal to c. not equal to

New Syllabus Mentals and Extension 1, Stage On

Answers

p42
1.a. twenty dollars b. one hundred dollars
c. fifty dollars d. five dollars e. ten dollars
2. $5, $10, $20, $50, $100
3. Tick $50 + $20 + $10+ $5 = $85
4. Colour 5 x $2 = $10
5.a. 4x$5= $20 b. 2x$5= $10 c. 10x$5= $50
6.a. $7 b. $30 c. $100
7. $50 8.a. $19 b. $73.50

p43
1.a. ten dollars b. fifty dollars c. twenty dollars
2.a. $31.80 b. $23.50 c. $68.50
3. 10c (1st), 20c (2nd), 50c (3rd), $2 (4th),
$5 (5th), $10 (6th), $20 (7th), $50 (8th)
4.a. purply/pink b. red c. blue
5.a. $71 b. $35.85 c. $60.80
6.a. Colour all - $115 b. Colour all - $90
7. 5 x $10 = $50, 2 x $10 = $20
10 x $10 = $100
8. $18

p44
1. $20 buys T shirt, $50 buys tennis racquet,
$100 buys scooter, $5 buys book.
2.a. $10.30 b. $80.65
3.a. $50 + $1 + 50 cents
b. $10 + $5 + $2 + $1 + 20 cents
4. 10 cakes
5.a. Colour $50 + $5 + $2 + 50c = $57.50
b. Colour $50 + $20 + $20 + 10c = $90.10
6.a. is equal to b. is not equal to c. is equal to
7.a. $14 b. $20 8. 5 x $20 = $100

p45
1.a. Colour 5 x $10 = $50
b. Colour 4 x $5 = $20
2.a. 50 cents b. 20 cents
3. $35 4. $95 5. $16.70
6.a. $83.50 b. $37.85
7.a. $5 b. $25 c. $5 d. $15
8. middle card
9. chips, sandwich, kettle (jug)
10. No 11. 7 x $5 = $35

p46
Extension 1. $1 2. fifty cents 3. 20 x 10c 4. $2
5. 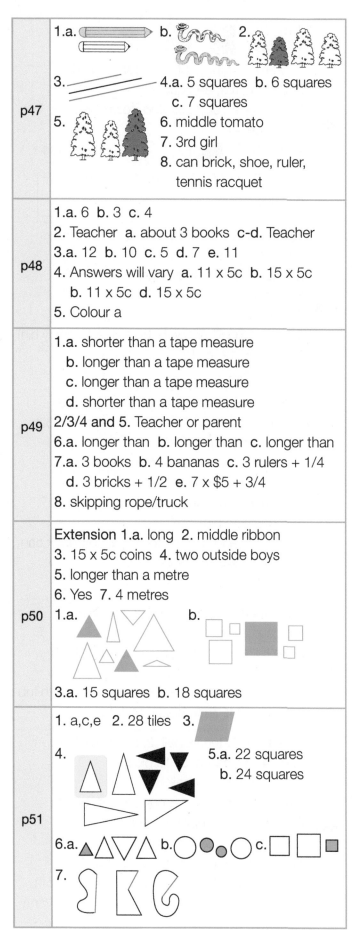 6. 20 cent coin 7. 40 x 10c = $4
8. One hundred dollars
9. $1.75 10. twenty dollars
11. $2 + $1 + 20c + 20c + 10c
12. $35.30 13. $5, $10, $20, $50, $100
14. 5c, 10c, 20, 50c, $1, $2
15. Yes 16. twenty dollars
17. 20 x $5 = $100

p47
1.a. b. 2.
3. 4.a. 5 squares b. 6 squares
c. 7 squares
5. 6. middle tomato
7. 3rd girl
8. can brick, shoe, ruler,
tennis racquet

p48
1.a. 6 b. 3 c. 4
2. Teacher a. about 3 books c-d. Teacher
3.a. 12 b. 10 c. 5 d. 7 e. 11
4. Answers will vary a. 11 x 5c b. 15 x 5c
b. 11 x 5c d. 15 x 5c
5. Colour a

p49
1.a. shorter than a tape measure
b. longer than a tape measure
c. longer than a tape measure
d. shorter than a tape measure
2/3/4 and 5. Teacher or parent
6.a. longer than b. longer than c. longer than
7.a. 3 books b. 4 bananas c. 3 rulers + 1/4
d. 3 bricks + 1/2 e. 7 x $5 + 3/4
8. skipping rope/truck

p50
Extension 1.a. long 2. middle ribbon
3. 15 x 5c coins 4. two outside boys
5. longer than a metre
6. Yes 7. 4 metres
1.a. b.
3.a. 15 squares b. 18 squares

p51
1. a,c,e 2. 28 tiles 3.
4. 5.a. 22 squares
b. 24 squares
6.a. b. c.
7.

Answers

p52

1.a.

    3rd   4th   5th   1st   2nd

2. 24 squares, 29 squares
3. Envelope 1st, book 2nd, towel 3rd, lounge 4th
4. b   5.   6. 28 squares
7. 14   8. 2nd , 1st , 3rd
9. Toilet

p53

1.a. 9 blocks   b. 10 blocks   c. 13 blocks
   d. 12 blocks
2. brick, book, ball, orange
3. a and c
4.a. 4   b. 3   c. 2
5.a. bin, wheel barrow   b. bucket, esky (chilly bin)
6.a. 11   b. 12   c. 15
7. 38 blocks

p54

1. fish bowl 1st, drink bottle 2nd, jug 3rd, can 4th, cup and saucer 5th, egg cup 6th
2. colander, net, funnel
3. pencils - pencil case, fish - fish bowl, shoes - shoe box
4.a. bucket   b. refrigerator   c. juice bottle
   d. garbage bin
5.   6. egg cup, coffee mug, soft drink can, sauce bottle
7. pot, tray

p55

1.a. kitchen tidy   b. cup   c. cereal box
   d. jam jar   e. match box   f. glass
2. kettle, esky, garbage bin, sulo bin, bath
3.a. 14 blocks   b. 15 blocks   4. 9 jugs
5. a   6. wine barrel, sulo bin, water tank, bath tub
7. tissue box, shoe box, match box

p56

Extension 1. tennis ball   2. a (11 blocks)
3. d   4. 8 glasses   5. 16 blocks
6. tree, log, tennis ball
7.a. apple   b. book   c. pumpkin   d. brick
8. car - heavy, elephant - heaviest, leaf - light, balloon - light
9. feather 1st, pencil 2nd, 20c 3rd, tennis ball 4th, orange 5th, cricket ball 6th, pineapple 7th, brick 8th (Answers may vary)

p57

1.a. brick   b. cricket ball   c. sand/water   d. truck
2. big dog
3.a. false   b. true   c. false   d. true
4.a. watermelon   b. crocodile   c. cricket ball
5.a.   b.   6. heavier   7. Yes

p58

1.a.   b.

2. True   3. 3 marbles   4.a. down   b. up   5. shoe
Extension 1. strawberry 1st, apple 2nd, orange 3rd, pineapple 4th
2. elephant   3. false
4.a. cricket ball   b. cup and saucer   c. brick
5.a. baby, boy, mother, man   6.

p59

1. Sunday - Wednesday - Friday
2.a. Yes   b. Yes   c. Yes
3. football, swim, lawns, paint fence
4. Monday   5. Wednesday
6. May 5th, July 7th, April 4th, August 8th, December 12th, January 1st, June 6th, March 3rd, November 11th, October 10th, September 9th, February 2nd
7. Picture 'c'   8. March, April, May
9. May   10. 31 days   11. December

p60

1. Teacher   2. Teacher   3. June
4. 30 days   5. 31 days   6. Student
7. September, October, November
8. March   9. 365   10. Teacher
11. January 31 days, February 28/29 days, March 31 days, April 30 days, May 31 days, June 30 days, July 31 days, August 31 days, September 30 days, October 31 days, November 30 days, December 31 days
12. 30th June   13. 1st May
14.a. Winter - June, July, August
   b. Summer - December, January, February
15. 366 days

p61

1. tie shoes/clean teeth
2. Teacher   3. build a house
4.a. 90 days   b. 92 days   c. 91 days   d. 92 days
Extension 5. 7 days   6. Tuesday, Friday
7.a. Yes   b. Yes   8. Saturday and Sunday
9. 12 months   10. 30 days   11. Autumn
12. September, October, November
13. November   14. five minutes

New Syllabus Mentals and Extension 1, Stage On

Answers

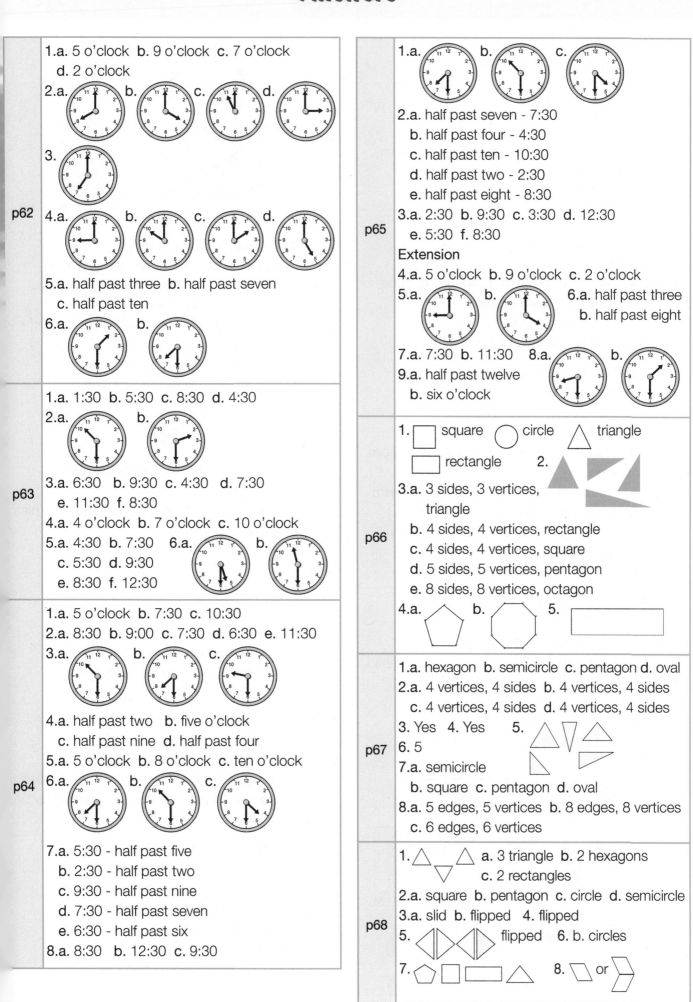

p62

1.a. 5 o'clock b. 9 o'clock c. 7 o'clock
   d. 2 o'clock
2.a.   b.   c.   d.
3.
4.a.   b.   c.   d.
5.a. half past three b. half past seven
   c. half past ten
6.a.   b.

p63

1.a. 1:30 b. 5:30 c. 8:30 d. 4:30
2.a.   b.
3.a. 6:30 b. 9:30 c. 4:30 d. 7:30
   e. 11:30 f. 8:30
4.a. 4 o'clock b. 7 o'clock c. 10 o'clock
5.a. 4:30 b. 7:30   6.a.   b.
   c. 5:30 d. 9:30
   e. 8:30 f. 12:30

p64

1.a. 5 o'clock b. 7:30 c. 10:30
2.a. 8:30 b. 9:00 c. 7:30 d. 6:30 e. 11:30
3.a.   b.   c.
4.a. half past two   b. five o'clock
   c. half past nine d. half past four
5.a. 5 o'clock b. 8 o'clock c. ten o'clock
6.a.   b.   c.
7.a. 5:30 - half past five
   b. 2:30 - half past two
   c. 9:30 - half past nine
   d. 7:30 - half past seven
   e. 6:30 - half past six
8.a. 8:30 b. 12:30 c. 9:30

p65

1.a.   b.   c.
2.a. half past seven - 7:30
   b. half past four - 4:30
   c. half past ten - 10:30
   d. half past two - 2:30
   e. half past eight - 8:30
3.a. 2:30 b. 9:30 c. 3:30 d. 12:30
   e. 5:30 f. 8:30
Extension
4.a. 5 o'clock b. 9 o'clock c. 2 o'clock
5.a.   b.   6.a. half past three
                 b. half past eight
7.a. 7:30 b. 11:30   8.a.   b.
9.a. half past twelve
   b. six o'clock

p66

1. ☐ square ○ circle △ triangle
   ▭ rectangle   2.
3.a. 3 sides, 3 vertices,
    triangle
   b. 4 sides, 4 vertices, rectangle
   c. 4 sides, 4 vertices, square
   d. 5 sides, 5 vertices, pentagon
   e. 8 sides, 8 vertices, octagon
4.a.   b.   5.

p67

1.a. hexagon b. semicircle c. pentagon d. oval
2.a. 4 vertices, 4 sides b. 4 vertices, 4 sides
   c. 4 vertices, 4 sides d. 4 vertices, 4 sides
3. Yes 4. Yes   5.
6. 5
7.a. semicircle
   b. square c. pentagon d. oval
8.a. 5 edges, 5 vertices b. 8 edges, 8 vertices
   c. 6 edges, 6 vertices

p68

1.   a. 3 triangle b. 2 hexagons
       c. 2 rectangles
2.a. square b. pentagon c. circle d. semicircle
3.a. slid b. flipped 4. flipped
5.   flipped 6. b. circles
7.   8. ▱ or ▱

Answers

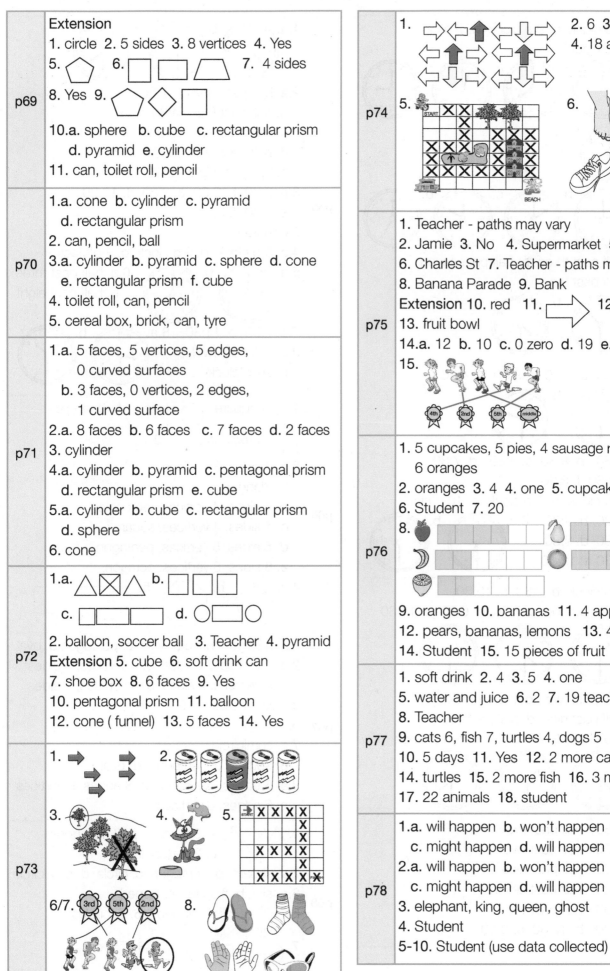

p69

Extension
1. circle 2. 5 sides 3. 8 vertices 4. Yes
5. [pentagon] 6. [square] [square] [trapezoid] 7. 4 sides
8. Yes 9. [pentagon] [diamond] [square]
10.a. sphere b. cube c. rectangular prism
    d. pyramid e. cylinder
11. can, toilet roll, pencil

p70

1.a. cone b. cylinder c. pyramid
    d. rectangular prism
2. can, pencil, ball
3.a. cylinder b. pyramid c. sphere d. cone
    e. rectangular prism f. cube
4. toilet roll, can, pencil
5. cereal box, brick, can, tyre

p71

1.a. 5 faces, 5 vertices, 5 edges,
      0 curved surfaces
  b. 3 faces, 0 vertices, 2 edges,
      1 curved surface
2.a. 8 faces b. 6 faces c. 7 faces d. 2 faces
3. cylinder
4.a. cylinder b. pyramid c. pentagonal prism
    d. rectangular prism e. cube
5.a. cylinder b. cube c. rectangular prism
    d. sphere
6. cone

p72

1.a. [triangle] [square with X] [triangle] b. [square] [square] [square]
  c. [rectangle] [rectangle] [rectangle] d. [circle] [square] [circle]
2. balloon, soccer ball 3. Teacher 4. pyramid
Extension 5. cube 6. soft drink can
7. shoe box 8. 6 faces 9. Yes
10. pentagonal prism 11. balloon
12. cone (funnel) 13. 5 faces 14. Yes

p73

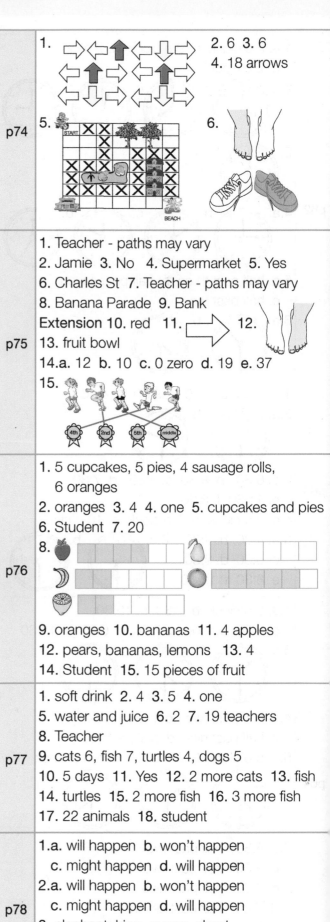

p74

1. [arrows diagram] 2. 6 3. 6
                     4. 18 arrows
5. [grid maze with X marks] 6. [feet and shoes]

p75

1. Teacher - paths may vary
2. Jamie 3. No 4. Supermarket 5. Yes
6. Charles St 7. Teacher - paths may vary
8. Banana Parade 9. Bank
Extension 10. red 11. [arrow] 12. [foot]
13. fruit bowl
14.a. 12 b. 10 c. 0 zero d. 19 e. 37
15. [children with ribbons: 4th, 2nd, 5th, middle]

p76

1. 5 cupcakes, 5 pies, 4 sausage rolls,
   6 oranges
2. oranges 3. 4 4. one 5. cupcakes and pies
6. Student 7. 20
8. [graph with apple, pear, banana, kiwi, lemon rows]
9. oranges 10. bananas 11. 4 apples
12. pears, bananas, lemons 13. 4
14. Student 15. 15 pieces of fruit

p77

1. soft drink 2. 4 3. 5 4. one
5. water and juice 6. 2 7. 19 teachers
8. Teacher
9. cats 6, fish 7, turtles 4, dogs 5
10. 5 days 11. Yes 12. 2 more cats 13. fish
14. turtles 15. 2 more fish 16. 3 more fish
17. 22 animals 18. student

p78

1.a. will happen b. won't happen
    c. might happen d. will happen
2.a. will happen b. won't happen
    c. might happen d. will happen
3. elephant, king, queen, ghost
4. Student
5-10. Student (use data collected)

New Syllabus Mentals and Extension 1, Stage Or